D1553364

NATIONALISM AND REVOLUTION IN THE ARAB WORLD

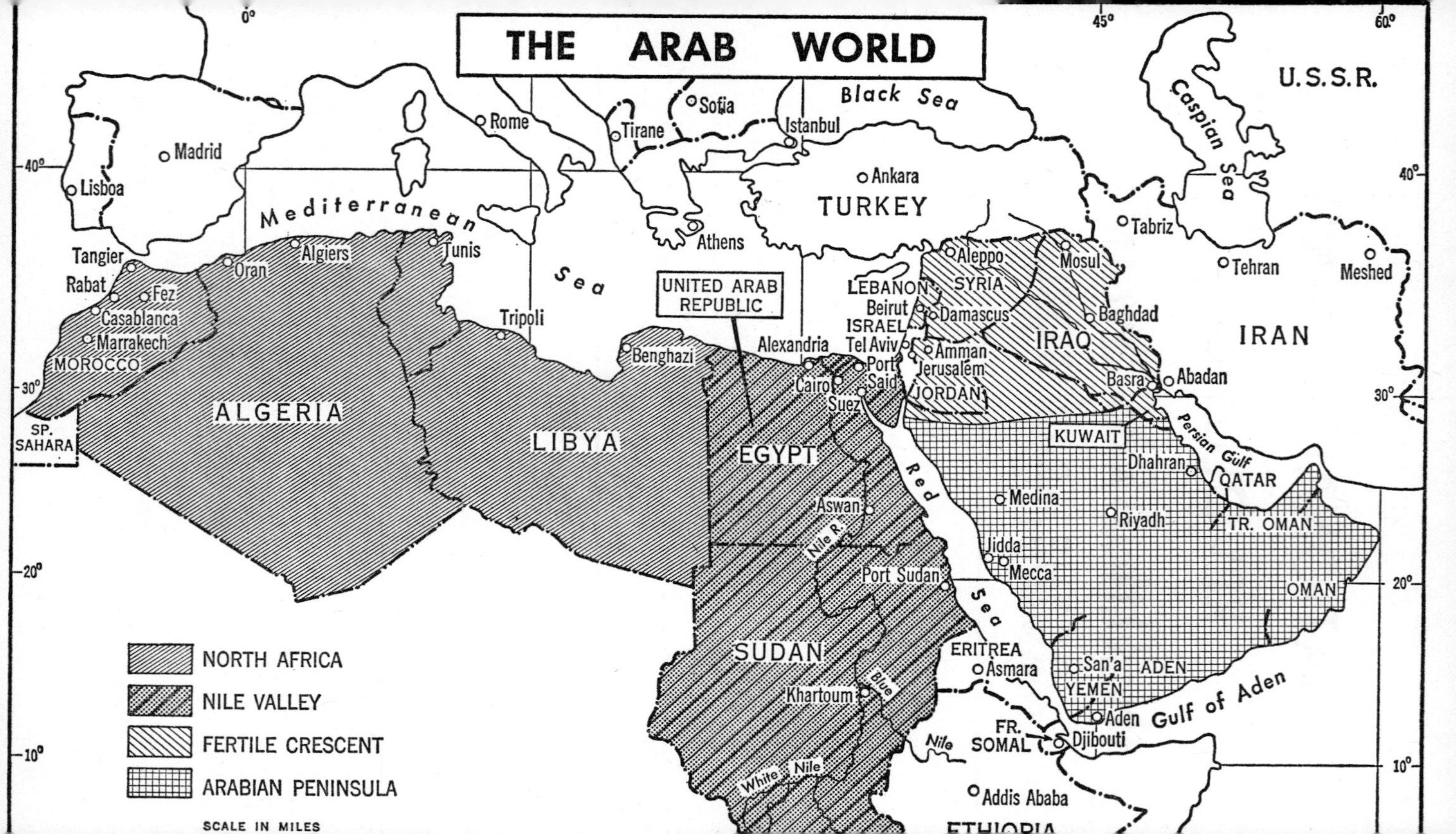
THE ARAB WORLD
U.S.S.R.
Caspian Sea
Black Sea
Mediterranean Sea
Madrid
Lisboa
Rome
Tirane
Sofia
Istanbul
Athens
Ankara
TURKEY
Tabriz
Tehran
Meshed
IRAN
Tangier
Rabat
Fez
Casablanca
Marrakech
MOROCCO
Oran
Algiers
Tunis
Tripoli
Benghazi
ALGERIA
LIBYA
SP. SAHARA
UNITED ARAB REPUBLIC
Alexandria
Cairo
Port Said
Suez
EGYPT
Aswan
Nile R.
Port Sudan
SUDAN
Khartoum
Blue
White Nile
Nile
LEBANON
Beirut
ISRAEL
Tel Aviv
Jerusalem
JORDAN
Amman
SYRIA
Aleppo
Damascus
Mosul
Baghdad
IRAQ
Basra
Abadan
KUWAIT
Persian Gulf
Dhahran
QATAR
TR. OMAN
OMAN
Medina
Riyadh
Jidda
Mecca
Red Sea
ERITREA
Asmara
San'a
YEMEN
ADEN
Aden
Gulf of Aden
FR. SOMAL
Djibouti
Addis Ababa
ETHIOPIA
0°
45°
60°
40°
30°
20°
10°
NORTH AFRICA
NILE VALLEY
FERTILE CRESCENT
ARABIAN PENINSULA
SCALE IN MILES

NATIONALISM AND REVOLUTION IN THE ARAB WORLD

(The Middle East and North Africa)

by
HISHAM SHARABI
Georgetown University

NEW PERSPECTIVES
IN
POLITICAL SCIENCE

D. VAN NOSTRAND COMPANY, INC.
PRINCETON, NEW JERSEY
TORONTO MELBOURNE LONDON

In memory of

FUAD NAJJAR
(1926-1964)

VAN NOSTRAND REGIONAL OFFICES:
New York, Chicago, San Francisco

D. VAN NOSTRAND COMPANY, LTD., *London*

D. VAN NOSTRAND COMPANY (Canada), LTD., *Toronto*

D. VAN NOSTRAND AUSTRALIA PTY. LTD., *Melbourne*

Published simultaneously in Canada by
D. VAN NOSTRAND COMPANY (Canada), LTD.

PRINTED IN THE UNITED STATES OF AMERICA

Preface

The man of action is always ruthless;
no one has a conscience but an observer.
—Goethe

THE PURPOSE OF THIS BOOK IS NOT ALTOGETHER A MODEST ONE. It is to analyze in a concise manner the forces that have shaped contemporary Arab politics both in the Middle East and North Africa.

For the first time in many centuries the Arab world is free and, in a certain sense, one. It now constitutes a single unit of investigation. Indeed, it is as difficult today to treat the Middle East without including North Africa as it is to deal with North Africa and ignore the forces which so intimately bind it to the Middle East. Furthermore, the final collapse of Europe in the Arab world and the rise of the "Arab Revolution" in the course of the last decade or so have created an atmosphere in which the dream of an independent and united Arab world has finally begun to acquire the aspect of political possibility.

Chapters I and II provide a general view of the political evolution of the Arab world in modern times and describe the general pattern of its response to Europe's domination. Chapter III discusses the process of passing from this domination into independence and the accompanying evolution of three main indigenous systems of power, the monarchical "palace" system, the "republican multiparty" system, and the "revolutionary single-party" system. Chapters IV and V analyze the postwar pattern of coups d'état and the impact of the "revolutionary wave" upon the development of power structures in the three types of states, the "revolutionary core states," the "monarchical traditionalist states," and the "intermediate states." Chapter VI provides an examination of the new "Left," concentrating on the ideology of three core revolutionary movements, the Algerian Front of National Liberation, the Egyptian Arab Socialist Union, and the Syrian Socialist Arab Resurrection (Ba'th) party. The last chapter is a descriptive survey of the "language of politics," with an analysis of some two dozen terms that constitute the essential political vocabulary in the Arab world today.

Part Two consists of four groups of documentary material—most of which are translated here for the first time—which illustrate the general discussion in Part One of political ideology, constitutional structures, and the coups d'état.

In rendering Arabic names and terms I have, for simplicity's sake, chosen to adhere to a simplified form of transliteration, using only two diacritical marks, the glottal stop ' (e.g., *ra'is*) and the guttural *'ayn* (e.g., *shari'a*). For well-known names and anglicized terms I have used common spellings (e.g., Nasser rather than Nasir, caliph rather than *khalifah*).

I owe special thanks to Professor Manfred Halpern, Princeton University, and to Professor William G. Andrews, Tufts University, coeditor of this series, for many valuable suggestions. I also wish to thank Mr. Hani Baltaji of Beirut, Lebanon, for making available to me a number of the documents translated here, and Mr. Jibran Bakhazi, of the American University of Beirut, for his kindness and help during the first phase of my research at the AUB Library in Beirut. I am grateful to Georgetown University for providing secretarial aid, and to Gayle Sharabi for painstaking editorial and research assistance.

Acknowledgments

Grateful acknowledgment is made also to:

Khayat's, Beirut, Lebanon (for quotations from Muhammad Khalil, *The Arab States and the Arab League*),

The Johns Hopkins University Press, Baltimore, Maryland (for selections from Appendix III; Majid Khadduri, *Modern Libya*),

The *Middle East Journal*, Washington, D.C. (for selections from the Tunisian Constitution, Autumn 1959, and the Algerian Constitution, summer 1963).

H.B.S.

Beirut, August 1965

Contents

Map of the Arab World ii
Preface v

Part One

I. Arabs, Arabism, and Islam 3
The Arab World. Unity and Arab History. End of European Domination. Political Consequences of Social Change. Islam and Political Behavior. Impact of Europe.

II. The Heritage of European Domination 23
Types of European Domination. British and French Colonialism. Pattern of French Domination. Character of French Domination. Pattern of British Domination. Italian and Spanish Domination.

III. The Systems of Power 43
Postwar Settlements. Negotiated Agreements. National Uprisings. The Systems of Political Control. The Patriarchal System of Power. The Palace System of Power. The Multiparty System of Power. The Single-Party System of Power.

IV. The Decade of the Coups d'État 56
The Disintegration of the Parliamentary System. The Seizure of Power. The Maintenance of Power.

V. Socialism and Revolution 67
"Revolutionary," "Monarchical," and "Intermediate" States. "Socialism" and the Revolutionary States. The Revolutionary Wave. The Monarchical Regimes and the Revolutionary Wave. The Intermediate States and the Revolutionary Wave. The Revolutionary States and the Cold War.

VI. Revolutionary Ideology 82

The New Left. Features of the New Ideology. Political Behavior and Revolutionism. Revolutionism in Transition.

VII. The Language of Politics 93

Fatherland. Patriotism. Arab Nationalism. Arabism. Unity. Nasserism. Federal Union. Independence. Sovereignty. Dignity. Honor. Traitor. Imperialism. Communism. Anti-Arabism. Opportunism. Reactionism. Feudalism. Progressiveness. Conspiracy. Revolution. People. Leader. State.

Part Two

I. Statements and Speeches 107

1. *Arab University Graduates Conference: Resolutions on Outstanding Problems,* 107
2. *Hasan al-Banna: On the Doctrine of the Muslim Bothers,* 108
3. *Michel 'Aflaq: On Militant Arab Nationalism,* 111
4. *Antum Sa'adah: On the Syrian Nationalist Movement,* 112
5. *Habib Bourghiba: On "Constitutional Socialism,"* 113
6. *Ahmed Ben Bella: On the Revolution, Arabism, and Socialism,* 114
7. *Hasan II: On the New Constitution,* 116
8. *Gamal 'Abdul-Nasser: On the Achievements of the Egyptian Revolution,* 117
9. *Fu'ad Shehab: On Lebanese Unity,* 118

II. Revolutionary Ideology: FLN, UAR, BA'TH 121

10. *Algeria: The FLN Program,* 121
11. *The National Charter of the United Arab Republic,* 127
12. *Resolutions of the Sixth National Conference of the Ba'th Party,* 135

III. Constitutional Structures 140

13. *The Republic of Lebanon,* 140
14. *The Republic of Tunisia,* 141
15. *The Hashemite Kingdom of Jordan,* 142
16. *The Kingdom of Morocco,* 144
17. *The United Kingdom of Libya,* 146
18. *Kuwait,* 148
19. *The Algerian People's Democratic Republic,* 149

20. *The United Arab Republic,* 151
21. *The Pact of the League of Arab States,* 153

IV. THE COUPS D'ÉTAT 156

SYRIA 156

22. *First Public Statement Following Husni al-Za'im's Coup d'État, March 30, 1949,* 156
23. *Second Coup d'État, August 14, 1949,* 157
24. *Statement of the General National Congress Condemning Shishakly's Regime, September 5, 1950,* 157
25. *Statement by Leaders and Members of Political Parties Addressed to the Chief of the General Staff (Brigadier Shishakly), June 20, 1953,* 158
26. *Statement by Captain Mustafa Hamdun on Behalf of the Aleppo Garrison Against the Shishakly Regime, February 25, 1954,* 159
27. *First Statement Following the Ba'th Coup d'État, March 8, 1963,* 160
28. *Ba'th Provisional Constitution, April 27, 1964,* 161

EGYPT 162

29. *First Statement Following the Coup d'État, July 23, 1952,* 162
30. *Ultimatum to King Farouk, July 26, 1952,* 163
31. *Three-Year Transition Period Declared, February 10, 1953,* 164
32. *Proclamation of the Republic, June 18, 1953,* 165

IRAQ

33. *Announcement of Coup d'État, July 14, 1958,* 166
34. *Counter-Coup, February 8, 1963,* 167
35. *Execution of 'Abdul Karim Kassem, March 9, 1963,* 167
36. *Provisional Constitution, April 29, 1964,* 168

SUDAN 169

37. *First Statement Following the Coup d'État, November 17, 1958,* 169
38. *Proclamations 1, 2, and 3,* 170
39. *Constitutional Order No. 1, November 18, 1958,* 170

YEMEN 171

40. *First Statement by the Yemeni Revolutionary Council, September 26, 1962,* 171
41. *First Press Interview with General 'Abdullah al-Sallal, Head of the Yemeni Revolutionary Council,* 171
42. *Provisional Constitution, April 28, 1964,* 172

SELECTED READINGS AND REFERENCES 174

Part One

I. Arabs, Arabism, and Islam

THE ARAB WORLD

To the Arabs the Arab world (*al-'alam al-'arabi*), or still better, the Arab fatherland (*al-watan al-'arabi*), refers to that vast stretch of territory from the Atlantic Ocean to the Persian Gulf and from the Arabian Sea to the Mediterranean. The terms "Middle East" and "North Africa" designate the two major areas of the Arab world referred to in Arabic as the Arab East (*al-mashriq al-'arabi*) and the Arab West (*al-maghrib al-'arabi*[1]). About one hundred million people inhabit the Arab world in its four principal areas—North Africa, the Nile Valley, the Arabian Peninsula, and the Fertile Crescent—or its thirteen sovereign states and semi-autonomous territories (of the Persian Gulf and South Arabia).[2]

The main concentration of population is along the Atlantic and Mediterranean littoral from Casablanca to Benghazi, then from Alexandria—past Israel—to Latakia, and in the riverine plains of Egypt and Iraq. The peasant population—about 80 percent of the total population—inhabits the lowlands and valleys surrounding cities and towns. The rugged highlands and mountain regions—the Rif and High and Middle Atlas in Morocco, the Aurès and Kabyle in Algeria, the Lebanon and Anti-Lebanon in Lebanon and Syria, the Jabal al-Druze in Syria, the Kurdish mountains in Iraq, the Jabal al-Akhdar in Oman, and the Yemeni mountains—are the home of linguistic, religious, or ethnic minorities. The vast steppe and desert regions, amounting to nearly 85 percent of the total land area (the Sahara and the Libyan Desert in North Africa, the Eastern Desert in Egypt, the Thamud and Empty Quarter in Arabia, and the Syrian Desert in the Fertile Crescent), are sparsely inhabited by nomadic and semi-nomadic tribes constituting about 5 percent of the total population.

Arab nationalists conceive of the Arab world as a single homogeneous whole and of the Arab people as a single nation bound by the common ties of language, religion, and history. In reality, however, there is more diversity and differentiation in the Arab world than there is perhaps in other comparable regions of the world.

To begin with, Arabic is not one but many languages. Classical or written Arabic is a possession of the educated minority. To the illiterate masses—perhaps 85 percent of all Arabs—classical Arabic is scarcely comprehensible. Colloquial or spoken Arabic itself consists of a number of dialects, which in certain instances vary from one country to another to such an extent that an illiterate Iraqi Arab will find it practically impossible to communicate with a fellow Arab from Morocco. Among the educated elite, classical Arabic serves as the *lingua franca* of the Arab world, but Eastern Arabs often use French in order to make themselves understood by Algerians or Tunisians, who are usually more proficient in French than in Arabic. In the Arab world today (and in language centers in the West where Arabic is taught) there are four or five major distinct dialects: Moroccan (Maghribi), Egyptian, Syrian, Iraqi, and Sa'udi (Arabian peninsula), which in terms of grammatical structure and vocabulary show marked differentiations.

Nevertheless, classical Arabic, the language of the Qur'an, remains a concrete symbol signifying to all Arabs their common heritage. Colloquial Arabic, though it is the language of life and daily communication, is everywhere considered a corruption of the pure classical and as such unworthy of serving as the vehicle of serious thought or the medium of literary creation. Thus classical Arabic is used in literature, in written communication, and on all formal public occasions. The development in recent years, especially in the daily press and on the radio, of a kind of simplified Arabic in which colloquial and foreign terms are used, has contributed to the rise of a new type of "newspaper" or "medial" Arabic which falls somewhere between the purely literary and the corrupted spoken.

Despite differences of color, race, and nationality, there has always existed among Muslims from Morocco to Indonesia a strong bond of brotherhood separating a "Muslim" from a "non-Muslim" world; Arabs assert an additional claim to Islam, attributing to themselves a special place in the Muslim world:

". . . the Prophet was an Arab, the Qur'an is written in Arabic, the Arabs were 'the matter of Islam' (*madat al-Islam*), the human instrument through which it conquered the world." [3] Islam served as the main binding social force in the Arab world during the centuries of its cultural eclipse and political decline; and in modern times it has constituted, especially in North Africa, a principal bulwark in the struggle against European colonialism and a rallying point against the challenge of Western civilization. To all Muslim Arabs Islam represents an indissoluble core of identity, a personal possession, and a communal heritage.

There exists a gap between Muslim and non-Muslim Arabs which has never been bridged. Internally this is a problem of special relevance to Egypt and the countries of the Fertile Crescent, where Christian Arabs were among the leading proponents of the Arab literary revival and of the movement of Arab nationalism. (Christianity was eliminated in the Arabian peninsula soon after the rise of Islam and eradicated in North Africa during the early phases of the Arab conquest.) The Christian communities in Syria, Jordan, and Iraq have not to this day been fully absorbed into the Muslim body social, and in Lebanon the existence of large numbers of Christians accounts for the sectarian structure of Lebanese political life. In Egypt the five or six million Coptic Christians have survived centuries of Muslim hegemony without abdicating their distinctive social and religious identity as a separate community.

Divisions within Islam—mainly the Sunni and Shi'i sects, but also a number of "schools"—have accentuated internal differences and in times of crisis greatly augmented communal antagonisms. For instance, Sunni-Shi'i mistrust in Iraq, though ostensibly latent, has acted as a major factor of instability in political life; Sa'udi power in Arabia rests on Wahhabism, a revivalist Sunni sect which dates to the eighteenth century and which views all Muslims outside the Wahhabi fold as having wandered away from the "true path"; in Yemen the centuries-old Zaidi-Shafi'i strife found vent in the civil war that followed the coup d'état of 1962.

In modern times Islam has experienced another division: the break between modernist and fundamentalist, reformist and conservative, westernized and traditionalist that has penetrated the very core of Arab social and intellectual life. Indeed, what is referred to as the "internal crisis" of Islam is, in its social and political aspects at least, this profound internal clash that has eroded inherited practices and beliefs and has given rise to a new generation of sceptical, cynical, and nonpracticing Muslims.

Yet it should be added that despite the retreat of Islamic conservatism in the past two or three decades, the idea of Islamic brotherhood is still strong, especially in those countries that have not been moved by the social revolution (e.g., Sa'udi Arabia, Libya, Morocco). In a political sense, Islamic brotherhood is basically pan-Islamic in orientation and therefore out of harmony with the nationalism founded on the concept of pan-Arabism. Between Islamic congresses and nationalist rallies there exist no means of contact or grounds for any genuine understanding.

It should be mentioned finally that when we speak of Islam as a concrete social reality and not merely as a theoretical system of practice and belief, we speak not of one but of many "Islams," as in the case of the Arabic language. Islam is one thing to the ulema, another to the western-educated, and still another to the illiterate masses. To the vast majority of the Arab world's rural population, Islam has long been transformed into a folk religion that varies from region to region. Regional customs, inherited superstitions, and varieties of saint worship have exerted a profound influence on present-day Islam. The impact, psychological as well as doctrinal, of the sufi orders and the other popular schools on the body of Muslim social and religious thought has not yet been fully analyzed. Among the educated younger generation Islam has become less of a personal faith and more of a national heritage, a product of Arab genius. Traditional Islamic piety, with its elaborate systems of erudition and scholarship, has receded more and more into the small esoteric circles of ulema, whose impact and influence on public life has been progressively decreasing since the end of the First World War. Even the opposition and strife between Islam and Christian Europe no longer moves the younger Arab intellectuals. An entirely new frame of reference has come into being which has transformed the Arab intelligentsia's view of itself and its relation not only to Europe but also to its religious convictions and its conscious Islamic heritage.

UNITY AND ARAB HISTORY

The Arab world has not constituted a single political entity since the brief period of Islam's expansion and consolidation into a Muslim empire during the seventh and eighth centuries. The dissolution of the central state began shortly after the fall of the Umayyad empire, which collapsed as a result of the Abbasid revolt in the mid-eighth century. The consolidation of Abbasid control (ca. 750-1250) created new centers of power throughout the empire. Effective Abbasid control broke down first in North Africa toward the end of the eighth century, as autonomous states arose in Tunisia and later in Morocco, then in Syria and the eastern provinces, which paid only nominal allegiance to the Abbasid caliphate in Baghdad. The ruling Arab elements were soon pushed out of power, first in the Abbasid state itself (which gradually fell under Persian and later Turkish control), and later in the Arab West, as the Arabized Berber empires of Almoravids (1062-1147) and Almohads (1147-1269) extended their control over southern Spain and most of North Africa. By the early sixteenth century, when the Ottoman Turks rose to a position of dominance in Islam, the Arab world was already in a state of disintegration and collapse. Syria and Egypt were conquered by the Ottomans in 1516 and 1517, Algiers was taken in 1516, Tripoli in 1555, and Tunis in 1574. Iraq, lying between the Ottoman empire and the rising Safawid state in Persia, was finally annexed by the Ottomans in 1639. In Arabia the Ottoman sultan laid claim to the Persian Gulf area, then to Yemen and the Hejaz. Central Arabia (Najd) and Morocco were the only two areas in the Arab world that never fell under Turkish rule.

The nature and pattern of the four-hundred-year Ottoman rule in the Arab world varied according to time and place. It declined most rapidly in North Africa, where it had never been firmly established. By the end of the sixteenth century effective authority in Algiers, Tunis, and Tripoli had passed from the sultan's representatives to military commanders and pirate captains. Hejaz, the site of the holy places in Islam, remained within the sphere of almost continuous domination, while Yemen, more distant and difficult of access, enjoyed long periods of autonomy. The Arab provinces which were most effectively controlled were Egypt, until the beginning of the nineteenth century, and Syria and Iraq, the closest and most accessible of the empire's Arab possessions, which were not given up until the First World War.

The ties between the Arab East and the Arab West (Maghrib) began to slacken as early as the end of the tenth century and the beginning of the eleventh. The East had always enjoyed a position of ascendency over the West, even though its political domination was short-lived. Toynbee compares the relation between the two parts of the Arab world to that between North America and Western Europe: ". . . Syria and Egypt may be equated with Great Britain and France, Tunisia with the Eastern United States, Algeria with the Middle West, and Morocco with the Pacific Slope." [4] In the nineteenth and twentieth centuries, with the French conquest of North Africa—Algeria in 1830, Tunisia in 1881, and Morocco in 1912—the isolation of the Maghrib from the rest of the Arab world was nearly complete. This was further strengthened by France's policy which aimed at creating in the Maghrib "an African France that would be an extension of the mother country." Travel to the East was severely restricted, and the circulation of ideas originating in Egypt and Syria was blocked. French domination transformed the Maghrib into an island neither truly European nor organically part of the Arab world—a cultural captive torn between its Muslim Arab past and its European-oriented present. *"Nous sommes Mussulmans et nous sommes Français. Nous sommes indigènes et nous sommes Français,"* [5] is the eloquent phrase in which Ferhat Abbas summarized the Maghribi dilemma in the twentieth century.

In the East, national awakening came much earlier and under quite different circumstances. Egypt broke away from the Ottoman empire in the early nineteenth century under Muhammad 'Ali's leadership (d. 1849) and became a major Middle Eastern power which threatened the existence of the Ottoman sultanate itself. The British occupation of Egypt (1882) served to pull it further away from the Ottoman-dominated Arab provinces to the east and to kindle the growth of a separate and intense feeling of Egyptian nationalism. Though Egypt played a major role in the movements of literary revival and Islamic reform in the last quarter of the nineteenth and early part of the twentieth centuries, it nevertheless remained immune to the impact of emerging Arab nationalism and the idea of a larger Arab fatherland.

It was in Syria and Iraq that the idea of Arab nationalism, embracing all Arabic-speaking territories, was born. Neither Syria nor Iraq had ever experienced a separate political existence in the past, but both had been the centers consecutively of the two greatest Arab empires, the Umayyad and the Abbasid. With the revival of medieval classical literature a new vision of Arab history, and with it a new self-image, began to take form. Still the struggle against Ottoman domination did not aim at overthrowing the caliphate nor at the establishment of complete independence. The striving for total independence did not take place until after the Young Turk revolution of 1908 had frustrated all hopes for an autonomous Arab existence under a decentralized form of administration free from the new government's policy of Ottomanization. While in Egypt the Ottoman empire was still viewed by both nationalists and ulema as Egypt's natural ally against British domination, the Arab nationalists in Syria and Iraq moved further away from the concept of Islamic solidarity, which the Ottoman caliphate represented, and toward independent Arab nationalism.

As late as the Second World War Arab nationalism really had only two centers, Damascus and Baghdad. Neither Cairo nor the Maghrib took any part in the Arab nationalist movement until after the end of World War II. In Syria and Iraq Arab nationalist leadership remained in the hands of the old elite that had formed secret societies against the Turks and participated in the Arab revolt of 1916. Their political ideas were general and vague, and they had no real awareness of social and economic problems. During this period the aim of all political action was to gain independence from Britain and France. Unity was the goal to be achieved after foreign domination had been brought to an end.

END OF EUROPEAN DOMINATION

The end of the Second World War saw political changes in the Arab world which were more radical than those occurring after the end of the First World War. Europe's dominance was shattered, and the emergence of the United States and the Soviet Union as the world's two super-powers ushered in the end of European colonialism in the Arab world as well as elsewhere in Africa and Asia.

France, though defeated in the war, undertook to reestablish its position in the Levant states of Syria and Lebanon and to retrench itself in North Africa. In 1945 it was forced to evacuate the republics of Syria and Lebanon, and by the end of the following decade, to grant independence first to Tunisia and then to Morocco. The Algerian revolution, which broke out in 1954, brought about Algeria's independence in 1962. Libya, which had been put under United Nations trusteeship after the war, achieved independence in 1951.

Britain's withdrawal from the Arab world was carried out gradually and without bloodshed except in Palestine, where the mandate was formally terminated in 1948. Transjordan was recognized as an independent monarchy in 1946; Sudan was granted the right to self-determination in 1953 and became independent in 1956; Iraq, already declared independent in 1932, became fully sovereign after the Baghdad Pact in 1955 stipulated Britain's evacuation; in Egypt the 1954 Anglo-Egyptian agreement brought about the end of seventy years of British occupation and the evacuation of the Suez Canal base; in 1961 the oil-rich sheikhdom of Kuwait was declared independent and became the State of Kuwait. By the early 1960's Britain's special position in the Arab world was maintained by virtue of its exclusive treaty relationships with the sheikhs and sultans of the Persian Gulf principalities, the Sultanate of Musqat and Oman, and the chiefs of the two Aden Protectorates.

In the postwar period another radical change took place: the domination of the old-guard nationalist leaders came to an end and was replaced in most Arab countries by a new type of leadership. The last great effort of the old leadership was to create the League of Arab States, a loose regional organization which joined together the six independent Arab states in 1945 (Egypt, Syria, Lebanon, Iraq, Sa'udi Arabia and Yemen).

The League fell far short of the hopes and aspirations of most Arab nationalists. It provided for closer political, economic, and cultural cooperation between the Arab states, but at the same time it gave formal recognition to the political divisions of the Arab world and confirmed the right of each state to complete sovereignty. Thus instead of providing a springboard toward Arab unity, it served to freeze the political status quo and strengthen the foreign-created political structures. The League's power and prestige sharply declined after the Palestine defeat in 1948, but it continued to provide a platform for meetings and discussion in times of crisis and to perform certain cultural and economic services to the member states.

The postwar period was, moreover, a period of violence and upheaval. In the Middle East the decade following the Palestine defeat was one of internal revolt and coup d'état; in North Africa it was a period of national uprising and revolution. These developments transformed established patterns of political life in the Arab world and ushered in a wholly new phase of political action and organization. The "liberal age" now came to an end, and with it laissez-faire economy and the supremacy of a privileged ruling class: in most countries parliamentary government gave way to authoritarian rule, free enterprise to the welfare state, and the multiparty system to the single-party regime. The ideals of social justice and radical economic reform, which had been circulating among the revolutionary intellectuals since the early thirties, now found expression in the policies and actions of the core revolutionary states.

Masters in their own houses, the Arab states now found themselves divided in terms of ideology, economic organization, and social policy. The "revolutionary" states—Egypt, Syria, Iraq, Algeria—stood opposed to the "conservative reactionary" monarchies —Sa'udi Arabia, Jordan, Morocco, and Libya. "Liberation" now signified freedom not merely from foreign domination and colonialism but also from internal "conservatism" and "reaction." By 1962-1963 "revolution" and "reaction" clashed headlong, first in Yemen with Egypt backing the revolutionary republican regime of General Abdullah al-Sallal and Sa'udi Arabia and Jordan supporting the royalist forces of Imam Muhammad al-Badr; later in North Africa, where border clashes between monarchical Morocco and republican Algeria almost led to full-scale war between the two Arab countries.

Thus the end of colonial domination in the Arab world, instead of bringing about a rapid movement of Arab unification, seemed rather to strengthen the tendency of each state to protect its own independence and to resist submersion in a larger Arab whole. At no time in the past was the feeling of Arab brotherhood so strong or the sentiment of Arab nationalism so warmly proclaimed; yet at no time in the past was the gulf between hope and fulfillment so vast and the realization of Arab unity so remote.

POLITICAL CONSEQUENCES OF SOCIAL CHANGE

The "atomistic" aspect of Arab society reveals itself most clearly in its patterns of social action.

All social action in the Arab world has the city as its center. Throughout Arab history the countryside and the desert have had a negative relation to the city. The city, the urban center, never really formed a *community* in the full sense of the word. Its inhabitants always lacked a civic sense (in the Western meaning of the term) and had no defined awareness of a common good. The Arab city itself had no tradition of municipal organization and no feeling of communal pride rooted in collective memory and experience.

The inner fragmentation of the Arab city reflects the same pattern that exists in Arab society at large. Today in most Arab countries the city inhabitants belong to two broad classes, a minority class composed of the economically well-to-do, the socially privileged, and the politically powerful, and a majority class composed of the masses of the poor, the socially underprivileged, and the politically powerless. Basic loyalties are not toward the *community,* but rather toward the family, the clan, the religious group or sect. The quarters of which every Arab city is composed reveal not only the economic and social stratification of urban society, but also its patterns of inner organization and its systems of religious and social values. The various *worlds* which coexist in an Arab city are not simply definable by the differentiations of social class or economic status, but are rooted in old familial, tribal, or sectarian grounds. Old hates and new grievances constitute the true well-springs of social and political action in these separate *worlds.* This is why in times of political upheaval the docility of the urban masses often erupts into startling acts of violence and cruelty. To the outside observer, sudden encounter with the extremes of social injustice and physical misery, which are the conditions of life for the city masses, produces shock as well as incomprehension. The indigenous rich, however, tend to be oblivious of surrounding poverty and the poor appear strangely reconciled to their condition.

The main urban centers of the Arab world today are: Baghdad, Mosul, and Basra in Iraq; Damascus, Aleppo, Homs, and Hama in Syria; Beirut, Tripoli, and Sidon in Lebanon; Amman, Jerusalem, and Nablus in Jordan; Riyadh, Jeddah, and Mecca in Sa'udi Arabia; San'a in Yemen; Cairo, Alexandria, and Port Sa'id in Egypt; Khartoum in Sudan; Tripoli and Benghazi in Libya; Tunis in Tunisia; Algiers, Constantine, and Oran in Algeria; Rabat, Casablanca, Fez, and Tangier in Morocco.

Only a generation ago travel from Damascus to Cairo or Baghdad presented an undertaking of considerable magnitude. North Africa was cut off from the rest of the Arab world, and only few Maghribis ventured on the hazardous and costly pilgrimage to Mecca. It was only with the end of the Second World War and the revolution in mass communication—air travel, the radio, and the daily press—that the Arab world was brought closer together. Today regular daily flights connect all the major cities, newspapers published in Cairo or Beirut can be bought in any Arab capital, and Arabic radio broadcasts are heard (now mainly by transistor) in every village and town throughout the region.

Yet the impact of these changes should not be exaggerated. While it is true that Cairo's Voice of the Arabs reaches the remotest villages from Morocco to Iraq, and that Egyptian paratroops can be flown to Yemen or Algeria in a matter of hours, the rural world to which the majority of Arabs belong has hardly changed in any fundamental sense. To this day the common man in Egypt still refers to the Arab countries to the east of Egypt as *barr al-sham* (geographical Syria), and one can safely assume that to the peasant of central Iraq or to the Moroccan villager of the Middle Atlas, Arab nationalism and Arab unity are terms which he has probably heard but which have little meaning.

Central to the process of social change since World War II is the rise of an urban proletariat in the larger cities of the Arab world. The formation of trade and labor organizations gained momentum with the expanding industrialization and its corresponding increase in urban population, which was accelerated by considerable expansion of elementary and secondary education as well as introduc-

POPULATION AND INCOME[1]

Country	Population, 1962 (millions)	Annual Increase, 1958-1960 (per cent)	Urban Population (per cent)	National Income ($ billions)	Five Year Increase (per cent)	Per Capita Income ($)
Morocco	12.3	3	19	1.54[3]	22	140[3]
Algeria	11.3	2.1	14	2.39[4]	92	219[4]
Tunisia	4.3	1.4	11	[8]	[8]	157[6]
Libya	1.2	1.9	15	0.56[7]	[8]	141[5]
Egypt (UAR)	27.3	2.6	24	3.25[7]	30	119[7]
Sudan	12.8	2.6	2	1.10[6]	24	91[6]
Lebanon	1.7	2.9	33	0.42[3]	13	263[3]
Syria	5.1	[8]	29	0.61[6]	2	124[6]
Jordan	1.7	2.3	[8]	[8]	[8]	[8]
Iraq	6.7	1.6	19	0.87[2]	69	138[2]
Kuwait	0.3	11.3	51	0.400[6]	[8]	[8]
Sa'udi Arabia	6.4	1.6	8	0.370[5]	[8]	[8]
Yemen	5.0	3.2	[8]	[8]	[8]	[8]

[1] Sources: *United Nations Year Book 1962; United Nations Demographic Year Book 1963; United Nations Statistical Year Book 1963; The Statesman's Year Book 1964-1965.*
[2] 1957. [3] 1958. [4] 1959. [5] 1960. [6] 1961. [7] 1962. [8] Information not available.

tion of universal military service. The other important aspect of this process was the transformation of the status of women, at least in the larger urban centers. The extent to which Arab society has experienced change in the course of the last two or three decades is nowhere else so dramatically revealed. The veil was abandoned in most Arab countries; Muslim women emerged from their centuries-old seclusion into public life and now compete on an equal footing with men in acquiring education and finding work.

These two major social phenomena, proletarian consciousness and the emergence of women into public life, have gone far to exert influence on social and economic life in the Arab world. But on the level of political action their impact was only beginning to be felt in the 1960's. Political initiative still rested with the elite, the small groups in each country, whether revolutionary or traditional, that held power and dominated political and social policy. The small urban proletariat still lacked political articulation and class cohesion; it constituted, from the political standpoint, a merely negative force that could react to but very rarely *act* upon political issues and events. Women were still outside active participation in political life.

Properly speaking, there existed no *public opinion* in the Arab world which could seriously influence political action or determine public policy. In the final analysis, the only truly effective agencies of political control were the two organized forces of the state: the army and the administrative bureaucracy. The bureaucracy gradually came to represent the permanent apparatus by which political power was bolstered and through which it was exercised, and the army the instrument through which political power was seized and maintained. Before analyzing the structure of power and the pattern of control under these conditions, it is essential to examine two forces that have profoundly influenced political life in the modern Arab world: Islam and colonial domination.

ISLAM AND POLITICAL BEHAVIOR

A genuine understanding of Muslim Arab political heritage should begin with a study of the *shari'a* (Muslim law) and the development of the caliphate. For our purposes, however, it is sufficient to point out only certain characteristic features of Muslim political thought and to single out the main developments that have exerted an influence on social and political organization and still affect political thinking in the Arab world today.

1. To begin with, it is important to note that in the Qur'an and according to Muhammad's teachings, stress is laid on external behavior, on the performance of social duty, rather than on intention or the inner life. Recognizing no distinction between the secular and the spiritual, Islam transferred to political and social organization the basically externalistic character of Muslim dogma. Thus from the early beginnings of social organization in Islam the realm between ideal and fact was never fully investigated and the opposition between the "is" and the "ought to be" only formally acknowledged.

2. Orthodoxy in Islam consistently stressed the primacy of the collectivity against the individual, of consensus against personal investigation; it supported established authority and set up communal unity as the highest objective of social action. Political organization had one aim: to uphold the faith and to safeguard the unity of the faithful. It was only natural that Muslim jurists favored political acquiescence and denounced rebellion under almost any condition. Conservatism and quietism became ingrained attitudes of Muslim political life.

3. The idea of "contract" was altogether foreign to the Islamic concept of the state; from the standpoint of its subjects the state was not their creation. In Islam (as in Hegel) the state provided the conditions under which the faithful, by adhering to the law, could fulfill their moral being. In Islam the "state of nature" had its equivalent in *al-jahiliyya,* the state of ignorance which preceded the coming of Islam; it was the realm outside society where the Law (*shari'a*) did not operate. As in Hobbes and in Hegel, sovereignty in Islam was not a trust bestowed by the subjects upon the sovereign; it was rather a right delegated by God and sanctioned by the prescriptions of the law. Pragmatically, the most important result of this dichotomy was the evolution of a system of control which set up repression and coercion rather than consent as the ultimate basis of power in society.

4. With sovereignty lying in God rather than in the people, it was only logical that rebellion against the state should be viewed not merely as an act of civil disobedience but also, and primarily,

as an infringement of the manifest will of God. The idea of absolute power required no justification; it was to be upheld in the state even when the sovereign was unjust. *De facto* seizure of power, which occurred relatively early in the history of the caliphate, developed its own system of legitimation based on the distinction between the institutions of caliphate and sultanate, with the latter being in theory wholly subordinate to the former and deriving its authority from it.[6] The Italian political scientist Mosca was probably the first to point out the inherent weakness of political organization resulting from this identification of religion with the state. He also drew attention to the meaning of *de facto* usurpation of power by the military commanders in the ninth and tenth centuries.[7] The Muslim jurists maintained that so long as the usurper of political power in any part of the empire recognized and enforced the law, obedience was owed him by the faithful. Disintegration of central power in the state did not bring with it a corresponding decline in the validity and authority of the law. On the contrary, political decline served to endow the *shari'a* with greater significance, for it became the principal unifying force of the Islamic community.

5. Separation of the "religious institution" from the "political institution," which first appeared as early as the Umayyads, led under the Abbasids and later under the Ottomans to the growth of political forms and practices independent from the control of the ethical principles of orthodoxy: the subordination, in other words, of the religious leaders to state authority prevented the Muslim church from playing the mediating role between government and governed which the medieval Christian Church played in Europe. (For many centuries the Muslim state was known to its subjects only through its soldiers and its tax collectors.) It can perhaps be maintained that the link between ruler and ruled was not reestablished in Muslim society until the rise of charismatic leadership in the twentieth century and the establishment of the secular welfare state.

6. Islamic political development was deeply influenced by the problem of succession which arose when the death of Muhammad left his followers with no provision for the procedure of choosing a successor. Primogeniture was introduced by the Umayyad dynasty in the seventh century, and adopted by the Abbasids in Baghdad,

but in practice the principle operated only sporadically and was never formally incorporated into the legal system of Islam. From the first Umayyads to the last Ottoman caliphs this lack of a definite principle of succession acted as a major disruptive factor in Muslim political life, greatly hampering the continuity of institutional growth and exposing the state to periodic upheavals that often led to violence and civil war. The cult of personality rather than supremacy of the political group dominated Muslim political attitude and behavior; assassination inevitably became a primary means of political action: a survey of the heads of state in Islam, from Omar, the first caliph, to Faisal II of Iraq shows that nearly nine out of every ten of all Muslim rulers died violently while in office.

IMPACT OF EUROPE

The Western impact on Islamic society in modern times may be viewed from the two main points of cultural influence and colonial domination—that is, from the standpoint of cultural borrowing by Muslim society and its consequences on the social, political, economic, and intellectual levels; and from the standpoint of Europe's military supremacy and political control, beginning with the French conquest of Algeria in 1830 and ending with the emergence of the independent Algerian republic in 1962.

The superiority of Europe over Islam and its immediate threat to Muslim society became evident by the end of the eighteenth and early nineteenth centuries. The core of Muslim society in the nineteenth century was the Ottoman empire, the seat of the caliphate and still the most powerful state in the Muslim world. Persia under the Qajar dynasty since the latter part of the eighteenth century was, despite political decline, independent and sovereign. Egypt, though autonomous under Muhammad 'Ali during the first half of the nineteenth century, was juridically part of the Ottoman empire, even after its occupation by Britain in 1882. Arabia, Sudan, and North Africa formed the fringes of the Ottoman heartland.

In its initial phases cultural borrowing from Europe was conscious and selective. It was necessitated by considerations of power, first in terms of military reorganization (Sultan Selim III, Muhammad 'Ali) and later in terms of administrative and political reforms. These were in large part measures of self-defense which were considered compatible with both the *shari'a* and the interest of the community. During this phase compatibility and utility became the two principles which governed Muslim attitude regarding what and how to borrow from Europe. On the technical level, imports consisted of goods and articles that were already "made"; the methods and techniques of making them were not considered among the objects of borrowing and were not adopted until a much later phase. On the level of institutional organization, the innovations which were most rapidly transmitted were those which were readily and completely formulated and expressed. Both ideas and goods were selected and treated as finished products and no concern was shown for the process through which they were initially created or produced. Thus it is not surprising that the least difficult and most rapid changes took place in the field of military reorganization and administrative reform.

As receptivity increased, cultural borrowing naturally extended beyond those areas prescribed by official order or delimited by military or political considerations. For example, in order to build an effective military and naval force Muhammad 'Ali had to establish technical schools, to send student missions to France, and to carry out economic reforms (required by rising expenditure) which had far-reaching effects on the social and political organization of the state.

Toward the end of the nineteenth and early twentieth centuries it became obvious that the simple criteria of utility and compatibility could no longer serve as the sole bases of judgment in the process of borrowing. Europe was much closer now and more comprehensible. It was viewed with awe and admiration as both the repository of power in the world and the center of science and civilization. The growing educated groups began to equate political liberty and material progress with Europeanization. Thus the borrowing tendency moved toward adoption of those aspects of European civilization believed to contain the secret of Europe's power and superiority. On the political level, the younger Muslim intelligentsia saw in the introduction of constitutional government the key to the solution of all the political and social ills of Muslim society. For a long time the ideas of August Comte, Herbert Spencer, and Gustav LeBon held sway over the thinking of the literate and the educated. For example, "evolution" (*al-tatawwur*) and "progress" (*al-taqaddum*) became two key concepts employed to explain all types of problems from political decline to literary revival. "Tyranny" (*al-taghayan*), however, was viewed not as the product of historical development but of social and scientific "backwardness" (*al-ta'akhur*); progress was interpreted not in economic or technical terms but politically, as the attainment of "liberty," "equality," and constitutional government. A shallow positivism dominated the minds of the most outspoken representatives of this generation.

Perhaps the most characteristic feature of the Muslim response to the intellectual and spiritual challenge which Europe represented at this phase was the *externality* of the interpretation of this challenge. It is significant that both westernizers and traditionalists, despite their differences, responded politically: they both aimed at reviving Muslim society, not inwardly, by means of a critical reformulation of doctrine and belief based on a radical searching of conscience and self, but by way of material advancement and political power. Europe represented to them the power and the glory which Islam had once possessed. The object of modernization was not simply to rebuild society; it was essentially to redress the course of history.[8] This is probably the reason why the late nineteenth century Muslim writers of Afghani's and 'Abdu's generation make one sense the presence of minds lacking in prescience and depth, of men who have more enthusiasm than insight or vision. As the impact of Europe increased, neither the religious reformers nor the secular intellectuals appeared ready or able to cope with the real problems with which Muslim society was now confronted. Change outstripped analysis, and response lagged behind established fact. When formulated, reaction to social modernization was broad and theoretical; specific and concrete problems were either denounced out of hand or altogether shunned. The profound transformation taking place in the lives of men during this critical phase was only dimly perceived and only partially understood. New ideas and new modes of thinking and acting simply proliferated in society with neither the ethical justification of the ulema or the intellectual sanction of the social critics.

Indeed, what strikes one most in viewing this period of "Arab awakening" is not the intellectual ferment and feverish activity that characterize periods of intellectual awakening and cultural rebirth, but rather a curiously uneasy state of mind dominated by suspicion, hesitation, and fear. Europe was already the enemy, and Islam, now unable to marshal its former might, began to succumb in the torpor and lassitude of withdrawal and retreat.

How to justify popular sovereignty? How to make a place for revolution? How to establish new bases for legality? These were the political problems at the root of the reform movement which both the religious and the secular wings were unable to solve. On the theoretical level these problems received no clear-cut treatment; they were eventually resolved in the heat of action, by violence and by political edict, first in Turkey by Mustafa Kemal (d. 1938), and later, more gradually, in most of the Muslim Arab states.

In adhering to the ideas of nineteenth century liberalism Muslim thinkers of the generation that saw the coming of the First World War failed to avail themselves of the arguments on which the political theorists in Europe from John Locke to J. S. Mill based their political principles and values, and limited themselves to proclaiming the validity of these principles and ideals. They saw only the functioning structures and institutions of the new constitutional democracies and parliamentary governments and failed to understand the political experience and philosophical tradition that produced them and which they embodied. The concept of natural law and the distinction between revealed truth and natural reason did not become fully clear until a later generation, when European-type laws and institutions had been adopted and the *shari'a* was already relegated to the background of political life.

The abolition of the caliphate in Turkey in 1924 was undoubtedly an act of seizure which at one stroke repudiated the Islamic principle of caliphal sovereignty and established by force the principle of popular sovereignty. The promulgation of the Constitutional Law of April 20, 1924, in Turkey, declaring that "sovereignty belongs unconditionally to the nation" (Article 3), represents a turning point in Muslim political development. This cutting of the Gordian knot served as the way out of the political impasse by directing attention away from theoretical debate to the concrete business of establishing new systems of rule and law in Muslim society. Henceforth, as these countries gained independence and constitutional governments were introduced, the central problem of political life was no longer of doctrine and theory, but of law and administration: how to devise the means whereby the rule of legislated law might effectively be enforced and eventually rendered supreme.

NOTES

1. *Al-maghrib* also stands for Morocco.
2. Morocco, Algeria, Tunisia, Libya; Egypt, Sudan; Sa'udi Arabia, Yemen; Syria, Lebanon, Jordan, Iraq, Kuwait; the Sheikhdoms of Bahrain, Qatar, Abu Dhabi, Dubai, Sharja, Ras al-Khaimah, Ajman, Umm al-Qaiwain, Fujaira, the Sultanate of Muscat and Oman, the Eastern and Western Aden Protectorates.
3. Quoted by Albert Hourani, *Arabic Thought in the Liberal Age, 1798-1939* (London, 1962), p. 33.
4. Arnold J. Toynbee, *Survey of International Affairs, 1937,* I (London, 1938), p. 499, n. 3.
5. Quoted by Jean Lacouture, *Cinq hommes et la France* (Paris, 1961), p. 24.
6. See H. A. R. Gibb and Harold Bowen, *Islamic Society and the West,* Vol. I, Part 1 (London, 1950), p. 31.
7. Gaetano Mosca, *The Ruling Class,* trans. by Hannah D. Khan (New York, 1939), p. 345.
8. See Wilfred Cantwell Smith, *Islam in Modern History* (Princeton, 1957), Chap. 3.

II. The Heritage of European Domination

TYPES OF EUROPEAN DOMINATION

Of the European powers, Britain and France most influenced the shaping of the Arab world's political character and institutions in modern times. They differed greatly in their approach to the countries falling under their domination—in the patterns of control, policies of government, systems of education, attitudes toward indigenous culture and institutions. And the type of domination exercised by each varied still further from one country or region to another. The structure of European domination took four forms.

First, *direct colonial* domination was applied by Britain in the Aden Colony, by France in Algeria, and by Italy in Libya. Algeria and Libya were put under direct and total colonial rule and opened to large-scale and unrestricted settlement by Europeans; the indigenous populations were excluded from participation in government and deprived of their basic rights. The Aden Colony, though administered as a colonial possession, was not subjected to systematic colonial settlement, and its inhabitants retained certain rights stipulated by law.

Second, the indirect and more flexible rule by *protectorate* was established by Britain in the Eastern and Western Aden territories and in Egypt, by France in Tunisia and Morocco, and by Spain in the Northern Zone of Morocco. Under the protectorate system foreign rule was assumed to be temporary and governmental and political institutions of the protected territory were preserved. Thus, in the Aden protectorates customary law and the *shari'a* were left intact and traditional forms of tribal government were continued; in Egypt the Khedival government and all aspects of administration and law governing Egyptians were preserved; and under French protection the traditional Beylical and Sharifian governments in Tunisia and Morocco were maintained (under the Spanish protectorate Sharifian sovereignty was also recognized). Effective control, however, rested with the representatives of the protecting powers.

Third, the *mandate* relationship devised by the League of Nations was applied to the Fertile Crescent area after World War I. The League gave Britain the mandate for Palestine, Transjordan and Iraq; and France was assigned Syria and Lebanon. In principle the mandated territories were deemed unable to govern themselves and in need of temporary tutelage and guidance toward self-government. The function of the mandatory power was to help establish autonomous governments in each of these territories and to prepare them for self-rule. (In Palestine the mandate entrusted Britain with the task of assisting the establishment of a Jewish national home as well as that of preparing the country for self-government.) Though throughout the mandates final political control was retained by the two mandatory powers, the checks and balances of the mandatory system as set forth by the League made it possible for the indigenous leadership to exercise a certain amount of political freedom.

The fourth type of domination, *"exclusive" treaty relationship*, was exercised by Britain in the Persian Gulf and South Arabia. On the basis of exclusive treaties with the various shiekhdoms of the Gulf and the Sultanate of Muscat and Oman, Britain undertook to protect these territories, handle their foreign relations, and provide them with aid and advice. The patriarchal chiefs recognized Britain's economic, political, and military interests in the area, and pledged themselves not to deal with any foreign power without Britain's consent. British control was exercised through a Political Resident stationed in Bahrain. He in turn was aided by Political Officers and Political Agents seconded to the chiefs of the various shiekhdoms and principalities.

BRITISH AND FRENCH COLONIALISM

Whereas France aimed, especially in North Africa, at centralized political control and assimilation, Britain's approach was to exercise power with a minimum of direct interference in internal political or social affairs. Britain at no time sought to *colonize* any Arab territory, either by emigration or by cultural assimilation.

Figure 1. President Habib Bourghiba of Tunisia delivering speech at the Arab Summit Conference, Cairo, January, 1964. (Courtesy of Embassy of Tunisia, Washington)

igure 2. President Abdul-Salalm Aref of Iraq talks to foreign correspondents in Baghdad hortly after the overthrow of the Qasim government, March 8, 1963. (Courtesy of Lisan l-Hal, Beirut)

Figure 3. President Gamal Abdul-Nasser of the United Arab Republic is surrounded by crowds after leaving the Cairo Broadcasting Station where he made a nationwide broadcast on the uprising in Syria which led to the breakup of the Syrian-Egyptian union, September, 1961. (Wide World Photos, by permission)

Figure 4. President Abdullah al-Sallal of Yemen receiving the allegiance of tribal chiefs at San's shortly after the coup d'état of September, 1962, which overthrew the monarchial regime in Yemen. (Courtesy of Lisan al-Hal, *Beirut*)

Figure 5. King Hassan I of Morocco reviewing Moroccan troops at Rabat. To his right is Marshall Abdul-Hakim Amir, Commander-in-Chief of the Egyptian armed forces. (Courtesy of the Embassy of Morocco, Washington)

Figure 6. Colonel Houari Boumedienne, successor to ousted President Ahmed Ben Bella, escorts Abdel-Hakim Amer, right, United Arab Republic Vice President, past honor guard at Algiers Airport. (Wide World Photos, by permission)

Englishmen served as administrators and soldiers but never became colonial settlers in any part of the Arab world. Existing political structures were carefully maintained and wherever possible authority was delegated to native officials and administrators. By contrast, French rule was direct (even at times in Syria and Lebanon). In Algeria, France pursued a line of total "gallicization," extending its control to education and traditional Muslim and tribal institutions; in Tunisia, and to a lesser degree in Morocco, it encouraged large-scale European emigration and facilitated the transfer of Muslim land to European settlers (French, Italian, Spanish, and Maltese). The French colonial administration was staffed almost wholly by French or European officials, and when France withdrew from the Arab world it left behind a French-speaking and French-educated intellectual elite, but few administrators or technicians. Britain, on the other hand, bequeathed a highly trained body of civil servants and efficient administrative bureaucracies almost wholly staffed by Arabs.

France withdrew from every country it controlled in the Arab world as a result of an uprising or revolution against French rule —from Syria and Lebanon in 1943-1945, from Tunisia and Morocco in 1955, and from Algeria in 1962. Except in Palestine, Britain withdrew gradually by granting partial independence in progressive stages—Iraq in 1922 and 1932, Egypt in 1922 and 1936, Jordan in 1946 and 1948, and Sudan in 1951 and 1953.

PATTERN OF FRENCH DOMINATION

France was the last of the European nations to abandon the crusade against Islam in the Middle Ages and the first to reconquer Muslim territory in modern times. Napoleon's invasion of Egypt in 1798 opened the era of European influence in the Arab world and initiated a phase of cultural and political domination which in the course of a century and a half effected radical changes in Arab society.[1] At mid-twentieth century the French colonial presence had finally receded, but its cultural presence remained strong: more than half the educated classes in the entire Arab world were French-educated, French was the predominant foreign language, and Paris was the cultural and spiritual center of most of the young Arab intellectuals.

French presence in the Arab world persisted longer than that of any other European power, lasting without interruption for over 130 years (beginning and ending in Algeria, 1830-1962). French imperial expansion, however, was slow: Tunisia was not occupied until 1881, nor Morocco until 1911, and in the Arab East, Syria and Lebanon were put under French control at the end of World War I. From Napoleon to de Gaulle, the attitude of France toward the Arabs remained paternalistic; the complex character of French rule, ranging from severity to compassion, from ruthlessness and repression to cooperation and reconstruction, is best exemplified in Algeria.

When France encountered Islam, first briefly in Egypt (1798-1802), and later in Algeria, Muslim society had reached its lowest ebb. To the French conquerors Algerian Muslims appeared barbaric and were treated by the first wave of settlers much as the American Indians by early settlers. Though Tunisia retained a higher level of social and political organization at the time of its annexation, it was viewed as an extension of Muslim Algeria. Morocco, medieval in social and political organization, and in a state of advanced degeneration when the protectorate was established in 1912, only confirmed the impressions and attitudes which the French administrators and colons had already formed in the other two North African territories. Even Syria and Lebanon, which by 1918 had already been exposed to European influences and had entered the first phases of national awakening, were approached with the same colonial attitude—by now solidified into established norms and patterns of administration and rule.

It is important to note that, except for Lebanon, all of these Arab territories resisted French rule first by general upheaval, then by intermittent uprisings. In Algeria, armed resistance under 'Abdul-Kadir al-Shihabi continued from 1830 to 1848, and the country was not fully pacified until the 1880's. In Tunisia a number of uprisings took place after the signing of the treaty of Bardo (1881), which established the protectorate, and the resistance—ostensibly broken in 1883—was carried on for some years longer by bands operating from across the borders in Libya. In Morocco, the protectorate was not secured until the Rifian rebellion of 'Abdul Karim al-Khattabi was crushed in 1926 and the Atlas Berbers pacified in 1931; Syria fought the French army at Maisalun in 1920, and rose in rebellion against the French mandate in 1925-1927.

Algeria

By the end of the first fifty years of French occupation, the Algerian Muslims had lost not only their freedom but also their land. As early as 1833 the *habus* land (religious property or *waqf*) had been confiscated, and in 1845 a law had been passed which divided the *'arsh* (communally held) lands and personalized property holdings, thus destroying tribal authority and facilitating the sale of land by individuals. The French authorities offered French settlers free transportation, land, seed, and livestock, and Algerian products were allowed duty-free entry into France. By 1851 over 150,000 Europeans had settled in Algeria. After the Franco-Prussian war in 1870 and the collapse of the Second Empire, Algeria's political status was linked more closely to metropolitan France. It was divided into the three departments of Constantine, Algiers, and Oran—consisting of the coastal littoral and most of the plateau and containing over 90 per cent of the total population—with prefects in each department.[2] The Sahara region was maintained under military control. A Governor General appointed by Paris had the power to legislate by decree, and was thus able to control the application of, or altogether withhold, metropolitan legislation. The departmental prefects were responsible to the French ministry of the interior and attached to the office of the Governor General, acting as his ministers. The European settlers gained in strength and were able to exercise vast influence on the machinery of government: they could determine policies, influence the enactment and execution of laws, and control the appointment of high officials of the administration.

In 1865, a law was promulgated which declared that "the Muslim native is a Frenchman," but stipulated that in order to attain full citizenship (including the franchise), he should adhere to French civil law. This meant that to become a French citizen the Algerian Muslim had to abandon his "personal status"—to give up the *shari'a,* thus renounce his identity as a Muslim. By 1934 less than 2,500 Algerians had chosen to do this. From 1881 to 1944 Algerian Muslims were placed under the administrative and executive system embodied in the *Code de l'Indigénat*. Under these laws, for example, an Algerian Muslim had to procure a travel permit in order to go from one place to another within Algeria, to secure official permission to shelter a stranger, to get administrative approval in order to give religious instruction. Punishment for violating the law was set by administrative officers whose summary judgments were without appeal. Punishment for crimes such as delay in paying taxes, speaking against the government, or holding gatherings of more than twenty persons, ranged from payment of fines to confiscation of property to indefinite administrative internment.

Shortly before World War II the Popular Front government sponsored a reform proposal (Blum-Viollette Reform Bill) which would have granted French citizenship to some 21,000 Algerian Muslims, but due to concerted opposition by the European settlers the Bill was never passed or even voted upon in parliament. The last attempt to solve this problem was the proclamation in 1947 of the "Statute for Algeria," introducing a new formula based on "integration." [3] It formally recognized that Algeria, while remaining "a part of France," had a separate "personality" of its own; all Algerian Muslims were to be granted French citizenship (*Français Musulmans*), without abandonment of the *shari'a* or their Muslim personal status; religious instruction was to be protected against state interference and the Arabic language taught in Muslim schools. The political provisions gave the Algerian Muslims the right to vote, but on a basis of communal equality with the Europeans, not proportionate to population, and thereby opened the way for their participation in provincial and local government. Again, the Statute attempt failed. Blocked by the powerful opposition of the settlers, its provisions were never fully or properly carried out, and the elections which took place in 1948 resulted in continued domination by the European minority. This destroyed the last hope for any lasting solution and reinforced the base of the revolution which finally broke out in 1954.

Tunisia

France gave full recognition to Tunisian nationality and to the existence of a Tunisian state under the protectorate. According to the Treaty of Bardo (signed between France and the Bey's government on May 12, 1881), France was to take charge of Tunisia's defense, foreign relations, and financial affairs; but two years later, the Mersa Convention (June 8, 1883) extended the area of French control to internal affairs as well.[4] Although the traditional hierarchy of the Beylical government was preserved, a separate French administration was established alongside which quickly acquired all effective control in the state. The Bey was reduced to a figurehead and all real power passed to a French Resident General.

Although the cruelty with which land was appropriated and the tribal system broken in Algeria was not repeated in Tunisia, French administration nevertheless put the European settlers' interests first and subjected Tunisia to "reforms" that were clearly not in the interest of the Muslim population. The *habus* land, though not directly confiscated, was made rentable in perpetuity under the so-called *enzel* right. In 1905 this land became legally salable. Individual landholdings became subject to registration, which simplified sale to Europeans. As land was bought up by settlers, the rural Muslim population sank into much the same destitution as the Algerian population. In the countryside, administrative control was strengthened by incorporating the traditional offices of *qaid* (local executive appointed by Beylical decree) and tribal *shaikh* (traditional chief) into the government administration, making both offices salaried positions and subject to the directives of the French *contrôleurs civils*. Though in theory administrative offices were open to both Tunisian and European civil servants, the Tunisians were prevented from occupying major posts until after the First World War. As in Algeria, the European settlers obstructed reforms granting Tunisians equal rights with Europeans, and held fast to their control of the political and economic life of the country. But unlike their counterparts in Algeria, the Europeans in Tunisia were unable for long to suppress the rise of Tunisian nationalism.

Tunisian resistance to French domination began to take shape just before the outbreak of World War I, and after the war became consolidated in the Destour (Constitution) party. Its demands were for administrative and legal reforms rather than full independence. In 1934 a group of young intellectuals split from the Destour to form the Neo-Destour party and within a few years appropriated the leadership of the nationalist movement.

Frequent and prolonged negotiations between nationalist leaders and the French government during the interwar period began to open some key government and administrative positions to Tunisians. After the war, in 1946, the Tunisian nationalists formally demanded the end of the protectorate and complete independence.[5] Settler opposition and governmental repression in the following few years only served to strengthen the nationalist position. In the summer of 1952 armed insurrection broke out and set the final stage for a Franco-Tunisian settlement leading to independence.

Morocco

The regime established by France in Morocco was modeled on the protectorate in Tunisia. When the Treaty of Fez was signed (March 30, 1912)[6] Morocco was an absolute monarchy under the 'Alawi Sharifian dynasty, governed according to the *shari'a* and established customary law. France recognized Morocco as a nation and a state and undertook, in accordance with the Treaty, to support the Sharifian throne and to uphold the religious authority of the sultan.

The basic structure of the sultan's government was retained; indeed, the feudal elements in Moroccan society were encouraged and the great families maintained their powerful positions. Unlike in Tunisia, no separate administrative structure was established alongside that of the sultan. Instead, a departmental system, run exclusively by French officials, was created as an administrative substructure. Official legislation and decrees were signed by the sultan and promulgated in his name, leaving him at the center of public life and at least nominally the source of authority in the country.

Extensive colonization in Morocco came late, for actual pacification of the country was not really achieved until the 1930's. At this point, major concessions were given to large French companies and state-owned combines. Unlike in Algeria, the colonizers were mostly lower middle class professionals who emigrated to Morocco to get paying jobs, mostly in business and administration. Marshal

Lyautey, the first Resident General in Morocco (1912-1925), established a policy of preservation aimed at perpetuating the social customs and traditions of the Moroccan population and protecting it from the transforming influences of Europe. (He instituted complete separation between the *medinas* [the native towns] and the European sections of the major cities.)

Lyautey's patriarchal policy of total one-man control was facilitated in part by the role the army played throughout most of the forty-three years of the protectorate. Particularly in rural Morocco and the Berber regions, the army stayed on to serve the administration after pacification had taken place.

Resistance to French domination in Morocco was almost continuous. It was not until the late 1930's, however, that the first political groups began to organize under the leadership of a handful of upper class intellectuals. As in Tunisia, demands were for legal and administrative reform. It took the collapse of France and the Allied landing in North Africa in 1942 to transform the call for reform to demands for complete independence. A formal manifesto was drawn up in January 1944 by the Istiqlal (Independence) party, formed just one month earlier, in December 1943.[7] French reaction to nationalist demands alternated, as in Tunisia, between partial concession and repression. Finally, in 1952, nationalist resistance went underground and open rebellion against France was declared.

Syria and Lebanon

In Syria and Lebanon, France was charged with carrying out "on behalf of the League of Nations . . . measures to facilitate the progressive development of Syria and Lebanon as independent states," and to draw up constitutions "in agreement with the native authorities . . . within a period of three years from the coming into force of [the] mandate."[8] Upon taking over her charges, France proceeded to reorganize the political map of the Levant. "Mount Lebanon," which was predominantly Christian, was enlarged by the addition of Muslim areas in the west, north, and south, and the new entity was named the Republic of Greater Lebanon (Grand Liban); Syria was divided into five distinct units, the State of Latakia (the 'Alawi district in the northwest), the State of Jabal al-Druze (the Druze district south of Damascus), the State of Aleppo (northern Syria), the State of Syria (the districts of Damascus, Homs, and Hama), and the Sanjaq of Alexandretta (the region west of Aleppo, ceded to Turkey in 1938).

Communal, linguistic, and regional separatisms were reinforced by these divisions and by the administrative policy which France now pursued. As in North Africa, force was often used as an instrument of political control—military action was taken in 1920 and intermittently until 1927 against Syrian rebels, in 1943 against the nationalists in Lebanon, and again in 1945 against the Syrians. Military rule was frequently imposed and the constitutions many times suspended; arrest, imprisonment, or exile of nationalist leaders were not uncommon.

The constitutions for Syria and Lebanon were drawn up by Syrian and Lebanese "notables" under the supervision of the High Commissioner and promulgated in 1926 (Lebanon) and in 1930 (Syria).[9] The newly established parliamentary life, especially in Syria, proved difficult, and friction between the national governments and the mandatory power was almost continuous. Elections were "arranged," and parliament, particularly in Syria, was frequently dissolved by order of the High Commissioner. During the Popular Front period in 1936 hopes were raised by an agreement with France that promised autonomy to the two republics; but the treaties concluded between France and Syria and Lebanon in 1936 were never ratified by the French parliament. The political impasse which was now created dominated the remaining years of the mandate. In 1941 Free France declared the termination of the mandate, but held fast to its position in the two states until the end of the war, when under British and American pressure France was forced to withdraw from the Levant.

France's twenty-five-year mandate over Syria and Lebanon failed to realize its purpose, mainly because the two countries were so vigorously opposed to foreign "guidance." The Maronites alone in Lebanon were not ill-disposed toward France, to whom they were bound by historical and religious ties. In Syria nationalist opposition was such that it became impossible to achieve even a modicum of political normalcy in which parliamentary government and democratic institutions could be established and given a fair chance to develop. France, on its part, seemed more concerned with establishing a position of strength in the eastern

Mediterranean by entrenching itself in the Levant than in helping the two states attain political independence.

CHARACTER OF FRENCH DOMINATION

French rule in the Arab world lacked consistency both in its long-range objectives and in its means of administrative control. This was in large part due to the radical political changes and upheavals experienced in France in the nineteenth and twentieth centuries—the July Monarchy, the Second Republic, the Second Empire, the Third Republic, the two World Wars, the Vichy regime, Free France, the Fourth Republic, the Fifth Republic—and the accompanying absence of centralized machinery for the control of colonial affairs. In the 1930's ultimate authority for France's overseas possessions lay in the two secretariats of the President of the Republic and the Prime Minister; the High Commissioner for Syria and Lebanon and the two Residents General for Tunisia and Morocco were responsible to the Minister for Foreign Affairs, while the armed forces with their separate administrative controls were responsible to the War Minister. In Algeria, the Governor General and the three Prefects of the departments of Algiers, Oran, and Constantine were responsible to the Minister of the Interior. Efforts were frequently made to coordinate policy and administration in the Maghrib and the Levant, but with no enduring results. The last efforts were made shortly before the Second World War, first when the "Higher Committee for the Mediterranean" was formed and later when a special cabinet post without portfolio was established.

In North Africa the most consistent aspect of French policy was the effort to perpetuate French presence through large-scale colonization and cultural conquest. Before the outbreak of World War II the number of European settlers amounted to nearly 1.2 million (by 1950 it had risen to about 1.5 million); of these a little over 100,000 lived in Tunisia, 150,000 in Morocco, and 990,000 in Algeria. The total Muslim population in the mid-1930's amounted to about 13 million (by 1960 it had doubled). By that time, the best land in the Maghrib, including most of the public domain, had passed through expropriation and forced sales into European hands. In Algeria the Muslim population was so dispossessed that in the rich coastal regions "a traveller who had been brought there blindfold, and had then had his eyes uncovered, might have easily fancied himself to be somewhere in the French Midi." [10] The Muslim Algerians, descendants of the former owners, had been reduced to a precarious existence as laborers and hired hands on the same European-owned land. In Morocco, though the number of European agricultural settlers did not exceed 3,000, they already possessed about 7 per cent of Morocco's choice cultivable land.

Despite the refusal of the vast majority of Maghribi Muslims to renounce their Muslim personal status to become French citizens, the process of "gallicization" made important headway. In the cities, especially of Algeria and Tunisia, French replaced Arabic as the language of the educated and became the medium of literary expression. In certain districts in Kabylia French became the vehicle of oral communication as well. Seasonal migration of thousands of workers, especially from Algeria, to the large cities and to France as well as obligatory military service, added momentum to the process of gallicization on a mass level. The object of French domination in the Maghrib, according to Toynbee, was "to absorb each territory—along its own lines and its own pace—into the French body politic and social." [11]

In its methods of political control, France relied heavily on the Roman dictum *divide et empera.* Religious, linguistic, and ethnic differences were encouraged and even cultivated, and regional, sectarian, and tribal loyalties were strengthened both in the Maghrib and the Levant. French administrators and officials belittled native competence and restricted Arab employees to subordinate positions. Though free from racist sentiment, France did little to prevent systematic practices of segregation and exploitation, especially in Algeria. In their contempt for the Arab and his way of life, the European settlers never took Muslim demands seriously. French authorities always underestimated the forces of nationalism, so were unable to accommodate their policies to nationalist demands. French cynicism in dealing with nationalist agitation is best demonstrated by their continued reliance on puppets and "Beni oui-oui" politicians and their simultaneous refusal to consider demands of the moderate nationalist elements. This resulted in every instance in strengthening the extremist elements which France had persecuted and imprisoned and with which it eventually had to negotiate. The reliance of the French colonial administration on force and repression served to weaken and eventually to destroy France's position, first in Syria and Lebanon, later in Tunisia, Morocco, and Algeria.

PATTERN OF BRITISH DOMINATION

Great Britain made its entry into the Arab world from India and the East in the early part of the nineteenth century. The first British outposts were established on the Red Sea, in Aden, and along the Persian Gulf. The opening of the Suez Canal in 1869 and the decline of Ottoman power in Egypt and Arabia led to the occupation of Egypt in 1882 and the beginning of British entrenchment in the Middle East. Until the First World War, British policy in the region was based on the preservation of Ottoman territorial integrity, and prevention of Russian expansion toward the Mediterranean and the Persian Gulf and German expansion into the Ottoman empire and Africa.

The collapse of the Ottoman empire in the First World War resulted in the extension of Britain's control over the Fertile Crescent area, which flanked the Suez Canal from the east (Palestine and Transjordan) and the Persian Gulf from the north (Iraq), forming a land bridge between the eastern Mediterranean and the Arabian Sea. The principal aim of British policy became the consolidation of her hegemony in the area without the exercise of direct control. Thus the interwar years witnessed the development of a system of imperial domination significantly different from that of France.

1. The first form of indirect control, established in the nineteenth century on the basis of "exclusive" treaty relations along the Persian Gulf and in South Arabia, was strengthened and coordinated with the larger complex of British commitments in the Middle East. Politically, the most important effect of indirect control was not only the preservation of the old patriarchal and tribal structures of authority and organization in these territories, but also their insulation for another generation from the political currents of Arab nationalism which other Arab countries had already begun to experience.

The same form of indirect control was established in the 1920's in Transjordan, which was included in the Palestine mandate but closed to Jewish immigration. Beginning in 1928, however, legal and institutional changes were introduced which led to the transformation of the patriarchal amirate into an independent constitutional monarchy by the end of World War II.

The only other political entity in this group to attain full independence was Kuwait, which in 1961 became the State of Kuwait. In 1962 a constitutional regime was established almost overnight and the patriarchial sheikhdom became a limited monarchy similar in many ways to those of Jordan and Libya.

2. British rule in Egypt and Iraq, the two most important countries of the Arab Middle East, underwent a more complex pattern of development. The relations between Britain and Egypt and Iraq throughout the interwar period were governed not so much by juridical or political considerations as by the fact of British presence in these two countries. British control of Egypt and Iraq passed through three main stages: (1) Military control, established in Egypt from 1914 to 1919, and in Iraq from 1917 to 1921; (2) internal autonomy, accompanied in both countries by the establishment of a constitutional monarchy (Iraq in 1921-1932, Egypt in 1922-1936); followed by (3) "Independence" based on a "Treaty of Friendship and Alliance," signed with Iraq in 1930 (which came into effect in 1932) and with Egypt in 1936. During the first stage all effective power was exercised by British military authorities aided by a small group of civil servants; in the second and third stages indirect control was exercised by the British High Commissioner, later the British Ambassador, and through British "advisors" employed by the two national governments in the administration and army. During the Second World War both Egypt and Iraq fell under more or less total British control, which was eased after 1943 and lifted in 1945-1946.

3. Three other systems of complete or near-complete control were exercised by Britain in the Aden Colony, in Palestine, and in the Sudan.

Aden

For almost a century after its acquisition Aden was administered as a British possession—first by the government in Bombay, and, after 1923, by the Governor General of India. In 1937 it became a Crown Colony, with a Governor responsible to the Colonial Office exercising complete administrative and legislative power, and a civil service and police force patterned along traditional colonial lines. After World War II restricted franchise was granted to Aden residents and British subjects living in Aden, and a Legislative Council with limited powers was established. In 1961 a ministerial system was introduced with the Governor acting as President of the Executive Council. The organization in 1955 of the British-sponsored Federation of South Arabia introduced new political patterns; and in 1963 the Aden Colony became a member of the federation and the Governor became High Commissioner.

Palestine

Though military rule in Palestine was replaced in 1921-1922 by a civil administration headed by a High Commissioner, military force was used intermittently throughout most of the mandate period to maintain political control. Attempts by the British administration to introduce elective councils and to develop local self-government failed, mostly because of the hostility and violence that dominated political life in Palestine as the pace of Jewish settlement increased. Until the termination of the mandate (1948) the administration remained basically colonial in character, with almost all key positions occupied by British officials aided in subordinate posts by Arab and Jewish Palestinians. The end of the mandate saw, on the one hand, the total collapse of government and administration in the Arab-controlled areas of Palestine, and, on the other, the complete assumption by the Jewish clandestine organizations of all functions of government in the areas under Jewish control. The annexation of Arab Palestine to Transjordan, first militarily (1948) and later juridically (1950), introduced the Transjordanian system of administration, and the two political entities were joined to form the Kingdom of Jordan.

Sudan

When Lord Kitchener was appointed first Governor General of the Sudan in 1899, it was a primitive chaotic country with few attributes of political or social order. After half a century of British rule a modern state was created and self-government attained (1953). During the first two or three decades practically all administrative officers, professional men, and technicians were recruited from Great Britain, Egypt, and Lebanon. In the mid-1930's a law was passed which prohibited the employment of a foreigner in any position unless no qualified Sudanese could be found to fill it. By 1946, 80 per cent of the civil service was composed of Sudanese, and by 1951 many of the senior positions in the administration were occupied by Sudanese officials.

Toward the end of World War II and in the period immediately following the end of the war, basic legal and administrative reforms were introduced and local self-rule was established. In 1951 a constitution was drafted providing a bicameral parliament and an executive council exercising most of the powers formerly enjoyed by the Governor General. The Anglo-Egyptian Agreement of 1953 ended the Anglo-Egyptian Condominion and granted Sudan the right to decide at the end of a period of three years whether to form a union with Egypt or to become independent. In 1956 Sudan chose independence. As the new state emerged it had one of the most efficient governmental structures in the Arab world, with a smoothly functioning administrative system, an independent judiciary, and a business-like parliament developing along the lines of a multiparty system.

British domination in the Arab world was characterized by its unobtrusive approach, by its reliance on existing political structures, and by its respect for tradition and established custom. In its policy, Britain was evolutionary and pragmatic, making room for gradual political change and for the development of new structures and institutions within the established political framework. In its method, Britain was conciliatory and compromising, eschewing the direct use of force and giving way before strong pressure without appearing hesitant or weak.

The British, unlike the French, had a good understanding of Arab nationalism and were more capable in dealing with it. They anticipated nationalist hegemony, and before the end of World War II encouraged Arab leaders to draw up the unitary schemes for the Fertile Crescent and the Arab League,[12] and to create in 1958 the Federation of the Arab South.[13] Perhaps the most salient feature of British domination in the Arab world was the outstanding efficiency and devotion of its officials and civil servants (e.g., Hogarth, Lawrence, Philby, Glubb, Cornwallis, Spears), who over the years played an important role both in determining British policy and in influencing political developments.

British rule in the Arab world functioned most smoothly in those areas where traditionalism held sway. Imperial rule and patriarchal government had much in common, and the two were able to coexist in relative peace and cooperation until the revolutions of the mid-twentieth century.

ITALIAN AND SPANISH DOMINATION

Italy and Spain were the two other European powers with footholds in the Arab world; in Libya and the Northern Zone of Morocco,[14] respectively, they ruled about 3 per cent of the total population of the Arab world.

Italian domination was basically similar to that applied by France in Algeria. Spain, on the other hand, mostly because of its long association with Islam, followed a softer policy which was in many ways similar to that of Britain in Arabia.

Italy's thirty-two-year domination (1911-1943) over Libya was perhaps the most severe experienced by any Arab country in modern times. Libya was subjected to a type of colonization which had as its object the total settlement of the country by Italians and the creation of an Italian "fourth shore." The pacification of the country was finally completed in the early 1930's by systematic and ruthless suppression, first of Tripolitania and Fezzan, and later of Cyrenaica. Mussolini's Fascist regime opened Libya to mass emigration financed and organized by the state. It was not until 1935, however, that the transfer of large numbers of Italian peasants to Libya began. With the coming of the war, immigration came to a halt, and by 1943 most of the Italian settlers were forced to return to the mainland.

Libya emerged from the war in a state of chaos and complete prostration, its decimated population wholly incapable of supporting itself without the outside guidance and help provided by the British under UN trusteeship. That Libya became an independent monarchy in December 1951 was chiefly due to the failure of the Great Powers to agree on its political future. In 1948 a four-power commission visited the country and unanimously declared it not ready for independence. Nevertheless, a resolution passed shortly thereafter by the United Nations Political Committee stipulated the granting of independence to Libya "not later than January 1, 1952."

The basic structure of the state was primarily the product of the British Military Administration which ran the country from 1943 until independence. The constitution promulgated in October 1951 declared Libya a federal state composed of the three provinces of Tripolitania, Fezzan, and Cyrenaica, with one federal parliament and three provincial councils. The form of government was monarchical, and in December 1951, Muhammad Idris al-Mahdi al-Sanussi, the head of the Sanussiyya movement and long-time enemy of the Italians, was proclaimed King Idris I of Libya.

Administrators, civil servants, and technicians in every field had to be imported, mostly from the surrounding Arab countries and Great Britain. Economic and financial support was provided chiefly by the United Nations, Great Britain, and the United States. In 1959 the discovery of oil transformed Libya almost overnight from the poorest Mediterranean country to potentially one of the richest, in terms of per capita income.

Under the constitution Libya's political life, like that of Morocco and Jordan (the other two constitutional monarchies of the Arab world), was dominated by the "Palace." But King Idris, aging and in poor health, from the start showed little desire to rule directly.

The Protectorate of the Northern Zone of Morocco was established in 1912, in accordance with the Franco-Spanish agreement concluded on November 27 of the same year. The partition, however, did not annul the sovereignty of the sultan over the Spanish-dominated zone. His powers were "delegated" to a "khalifa" in Tetuan who held the same powers and enjoyed the same privileges *vis-à-vis* the Spanish High Commissioner as did the sultan *vis-à-vis* the French Resident General. A mixed system of administration composed of Spanish and Moroccan officials, preserved local self-rule but also strengthened the supervisory control of the central government. Spanish policy was essentially nonassimilative in character, and political control largely indirect. The internal upheavals in Spain and the changes of political regimes during the interwar period (from monarchy to republic to dictatorship) prevented the development of consistent administrative policies in the Northern Zone and greatly obstructed its economic development.

The third administrative zone in Morocco, the Tangier enclave, was given a "special character" in accordance with the Treaty of Fez (Article 1), confirmed by the Franco-Spanish agreement of November 27, 1912. The international regime in Tangier was formally agreed upon after World War I by France, Spain, and Great Britain (1923), and was joined in 1928 by Italy and Portugal. The "Statute," however, was not put into effect until after World War II, when the city actually gained its international status and its administration was placed under the supervision of the consuls of the signatory powers. The sultan's sovereignty was recognized by the appointment of a Representative, *mandub,* who was responsible for the affairs of the Moroccan population. With the independence of Morocco both the Spanish Zone and the International City of Tangier reverted directly to the sultan and in 1957 were formally incorporated into the Kingdom of Morocco.

NOTES

1. Albert Hourani, *Arabic Thought in the Liberal Age, 1798-1939* (London, 1962), pp. 49-66.
2. For a brief survey of administrative development see P. Passeron, "L'évolution des institutions publiques de l'Algérie," *Algérie 54* (Paris, 1954), pp. 15-30.
3. For text of statute see Paul-Émile Sarrasin, *La Crise Algérienne* (Paris, 1949), App. XVI.
4. See Charles F. Gallagher, *The United States and North Africa* (Cambridge, Mass., 1963), pp. 71-72.
5. For text of nationalist demands see Abdul Hamid al-Batriq, *The Arab Nation* [in Arabic] (Cairo, n.d.), pp. 159-160.
6. See Alal al-Fassi, *The Independence Movements of Arab North Africa*; trans. Hazem Zaki Nuseibeh (Washington, D.C., 1954), pp. 86-87.
7. For text of manifesto see Alal al-Fassi, *ibid.,* pp. 215-217.
8. For text of League of Nations mandate see Helen Davies, *Constitutions, Electoral Laws, Treaties of States in the Near and Middle East* (Durham, N.C., 1953), pp. 283-290.
9. Text of Lebanese constitution in Helen Davies, *ibid.,* pp. 291-305; text of Syrian constitution in *Oriente Moderno* (December 1930), pp. 601-607.
10. Arnold J. Toynbee, *Survey of International Affairs, 1937* (London, 1938), I, p. 493.
11. *Ibid.,* I, p. 541.
12. Texts in J. C. Hurewitz, *Diplomacy of the Near and Middle East* (Princeton, N.J., 1956), II, Docs.

13. See H. B. Sharabi, *Governments and Politics of the Middle East in the Twentieth Century* (Princeton, N.J., 1962), p. 265.

14. Spain also held other territories which were not handed back to Morocco after independence and to which Morocco lays claim. These include the so-called presidios, the cities of Ceuta and Melilla, on the Mediterranean coast; the 600-square-mile enclave of Ifni on the Atlantic coast; and Rio de Oro (Spanish Sahara).

III. The Systems of Power

THE CHARACTER OF THE CONTEMPORARY ARAB SECULAR NATION-states and the manner in which their institutional and administrative structures were so radically transformed over the last forty years were chiefly determined by the experience of European domination. Each of the thirteen independent Arab states stepped into independence as a result of either a general postwar settlement (Sa'udi Arabia, Yemen, and Libya), negotiated agreement (Jordan, Sudan, and Kuwait), or national uprising (Egypt, Iraq, Lebanon, Syria, Tunisia, Morocco, and Algeria). Before analyzing the general political patterns which developed after independence, it is essential first to outline the circumstances under which foreign rule was ended (or withheld, as in the case of the first group).

POSTWAR SETTLEMENTS

Of the three traditionalist monarchies in the first group, Sa'udi Arabia and Yemen came into being as a result of favorable international conditions prevailing at the end of the First World War, and Libya at the end of the Second World War. The politico-religious leadership of the predominant religious movement in each of the three countries gained ascendancy and assumed political control—the Wahhabi in Sa'udi Arabia, the Zaidi in Yemen, and the Sanussi in Libya.

Wahhabism had been reestablished in central Arabia (Najd) shortly before World War I under the leadership of 'Abdul-'Aziz Ibn Sa'ud (d. 1953); after the war his sultanate had expanded to include the provinces of Ha'il, Hijaz, and 'Asir, and by the time the peace settlement was concluded and spheres of influence were established among the powers, had already been firmly consolidated as a state. The new regime's control of central and eastern Arabia as well as Hijaz and the Holy Places, represented, from Britain's point of view, a center of stability in the Middle East. In the course of the 1920's Great Britain and other European powers, including Bolshevik Russia, recognized the Sa'udi state, which was formally proclaimed the Kingdom of Sa'udi Arabia in 1932. It was the first Arab country in the twentieth century to become fully independent and sovereign.[1]

Yemen had led a semi-autonomous existence under Ottoman sovereignty until the end of World War I and during the war had declared itself on the side of Turkey. In 1918, with the collapse of the Ottoman empire, the head of the Zaidi order, Imam Yahya (d. 1948), declared himself king of the Mutawkkilite Kingdom of Yemen. Britain, long since established in Aden and the protectorates to the south and east of the new kingdom, considered Yemen an archaic state with no strategic or political value. Though recognized by Russia and Italy in the 1920's, its existence passed almost unnoticed by most of the other powers (American diplomatic representation was not established until after World War II). Yemen became independent by default and its continued existence as a sovereign state as well as its medieval political structure were preserved by isolation from the rest of the world.[2]

Libya at the end of the Second World War was, as already noted, in a state of total prostration and incapable politically and economically of independent existence. Her independence was the direct product of the great powers' inability to agree on a system of protection or tutelage to replace Britain's *de facto* control. The United Nations resolution granting Libya immediate independence was not a solution, but a way out of an international impasse. The establishment of a monarchial regime under the Sanussi dynasty and its organization along federal lines were in large part the result of these circumstances.[3]

NEGOTIATED AGREEMENTS

The Kingdom of Jordan, the Republic of Sudan, and the State of Kuwait acquired sovereign statehood as a result of negotiated agreements with Great Britain. Jordan and Sudan had never existed as separate political entities before falling under British control (1922 and 1899, respectively) and both proceeded gradually from total control under colonial administration to self-government.

Kuwait, under the "exclusive" treaty relationship with Great Britain since 1899, had existed as an autonomous sheikhdom and maintained its internal autonomy until the automatic expiration of the treaty in 1961.[4] The absolute control of the Al Sabah family and the patriarchal structure of the sheikhdom had been bolstered by Great Britain and emerged intact with independence.

In Jordan, despite gradual constitutional development which by 1946 had theoretically transformed the amirate into a constitutional monarchy,[5] the ascendancy of the Hashimite monarchy and the patriarchal form of government, especially under King 'Abdullah (d. 1951), remained. Jordan's independence, unlike that of either Sudan or Kuwait, was qualified by the country's reliance on financial aid from Great Britain and by the latter's right to maintain military bases on Jordanian soil.

Sudan, on the other hand, was able to achieve unqualified independence and to free itself from commitment to either Britain or Egypt.[6] In both Sudan and Jordan, the peaceful transition into independence allowed the daily routine of government to proceed without interruption and enabled the basic administrative and institutional structures to emerge practically unchanged.

NATIONAL UPRISINGS

The most important changes occurred in those countries which broke with the colonial power by armed uprising—most of the states of the Arab world, comprising over three quarters of the total Arab population. Uprising must be distinguished from coup d'état in that *a coup is sudden seizure of power by a small group of conspirators, whereas uprising has the character of a national revolt, committing a certain proportion of the population in armed resistance to the established center of power.* In modern times national uprisings in the Arab world have taken place *only against foreign rule, never against a national government.* Overthrow of a national government has *in every instance been in the form of a coup d'état, never of a popular uprising.*[7] (We shall analyze revolt by coup d'état in the next chapter.)

The Arab uprisings in the twentieth century took place against all the European powers exercising control in the Arab world—Britain, France, Italy, and Spain. The outcome of these uprisings as well as their character and duration varied greatly from one country and from one period to another. The Egyptian and Iraqi uprisings of 1919 and 1920 were the first popular movements of resistance in the twentieth century to lead to tangible political results. In Egypt the British protectorate was terminated (1922) and a constitutional monarchy established;[8] in Iraq the mandatory regime was drastically altered and the Hashimite monarchy established,[9] developments which dominated political life in both countries until the military coups of 1952 (Egypt) and 1958 (Iraq) brought an end to the monarchical regimes and established military control.

Uprisings in the mid-1920's in Spanish Morocco ('Abdul Karim al-Khattabi), in Libya ('Umar al-Mukhtar), and in Syria were crushed without immediate issue. Later, uprisings in Lebanon (1943) and Syria (1945) resulted in the complete and unconditional evacuation of French troops and their emergence as completely sovereign and independent republics. In 1947 Zionist terrorism contributed to the termination of the Palestine mandate by Britain, and the emergence of Israel and Jordan.

In the post-World War II period the scene of uprising shifted to North Africa. In Tunisia and Morocco national resistance (1952-1955) resulted in the end of French domination and the achievement of complete independence. In Tunisia it left the Neo-Destour party with exclusive control of power in the state and terminated the ascendency of the traditional Beylical monarchy.[10] In Morocco, on the other hand, the uprising consolidated the monarchy, which emerged as the center of real power in the state, while the Istiqlal party assumed a subordinate place.[11]

The uprising in Algeria (1954-1962) constituted a total revolution which had no parallel in the Arab world. Its consequences were the most drastic of all Arab uprisings—politically, socially, and economically. The result of the revolution was not only the final relinquishment by France of its claim to Algeria, but also the creation in 1962 of a new society, with a wholly new system of government and economic organization.

THE SYSTEMS OF POLITICAL CONTROL

The withdrawal of European domination from the Arab world initiated a new phase of political development which can only partially be attributed to the process of "westernization." A description of the structure and mechanism of Arab politics in the twentieth century is not sufficient if classified in terms of the formal categories of "democratic" governments and "dictatorships," "secular" and "theocratic" states, western-type republics and traditional monarchies, for the realities of power lie beneath the trappings of government and the outward forms of institutional organization. In terms of the systems of domination, patterns of control, and sources and claims to legitimation, four systems of power have emerged which can be classified as follows: the *patriarchal system,* the *"palace" system,* the *multiparty system,* and the *single-party system.*[12]

THE PATRIARCHAL SYSTEM OF POWER

In its purest form the patriarchal system of power is best represented by the states, sultanates, and sheikhdoms of the Arabian peninsula, of which the most important are Sa'udi Arabia, Kuwait, and, until 1962, Yemen. Although Yemen until the military coup d'état of 1962 was able under Zaidi hegemony to preserve almost intact inherited practices and forms which date to medieval times, Sa'udi Arabia and Kuwait experienced significant political and social changes after the discovery of oil and the influx of large numbers of workers and technicians from surrounding Arab countries and the West. Yet in all three societies, the fundamental attributes of the patriarchal system of power are the same. The head of the community is also the head of the state; he is the center of all power; his will is supreme, delimited only by the prescription of the *shari'a* and established custom. Under this system of power independent legislation is impossible, since the *shari'a* and inherited tradition are the only valid basis of legality for society and the state. Patriarchal government is simple and direct, despite the introduction, as in Sa'udi Arabia and Kuwait, of certain Western-type administrative structures. Power is neither divided nor fully delegated; government officials merely carry out the ruler's will. The key administrative positions under patriarchal rule are occupied by brothers, cousins, retainers, and servants, rather than by trained administrators and technicians selected on the basis of skill, training, or specialization. The basic character of the center of power under the patriarchal system is essentially that of the head of a household. Family ties, personal loyalties, and custom dominate public behavior as they do private life. The subjects of the patriarchal state have no separate or independent rights as individual citizens; they constitute the *ra'iyya* (folk) which the patriarchal ruler shepherds, protects, and looks after. The ruler and his family do not merely dominate the state but in a very real sense own it. The Sa'udi princes, the Al Sabah shiekhs, and, until 1962, the Zaidi Imam's family occupied almost all the important positions in the government, and each had his alloted share of the state's income. Used broadly, the meaning of Weber's "family-state" (*Geschlechterstaat*) is very well illustrated by the social structure and system of government of these patriarchal states.

The breakdown of the patriarchal system of power can take place under any one of three conditions: (1) conflict within the ruling family leading to the loss of effective control by the family; (2) military overthrow of the ruler by internal forces with or without outside support; (3) political reform leading to popular representation and eventually to the disintegration of the traditional bases of patriarchal control.

THE PALACE SYSTEM OF POWER

The "Palace" system of power evolved in Egypt and Iraq, where the first modern constitutional monarchies were established shortly after World War I. Following the end of the Second World War three similar regimes came into being, in Jordan, Libya, and Morocco. The pattern of Palace control emerged in each of them with slight variations occasioned by differences in political background, social structure, and the circumstances under which the palace system came into being.

The term Palace means here the institution of monarchy, the group or groups that represent and serve it, and the person of the king. Palace power may be wielded by the king directly, as in the case of 'Abdullah of Jordan and Hassan II of Morocco, or by a Palace group of politicians, as in Iraq during the reign of Faisal II.

The most obvious aspect of this system of control is that the powers actually exercised by the Palace always exceed those granted under the constitution. In this sense, there has never been a limited constitutional monarchy in the Arab world. The most direct manner in which Palace power expresses itself is through domination of parliament and parliamentary elections. In all monarchical regimes Palace pressure has always been used to influence the outcome of elections, and seldom has the opposition been able to gain control of parliament and to oppose the Palace on an equal footing. In Egypt under the monarchy, Great Britain was able to play the Wafd party against the Palace, and thus to gain a certain influence on both. In Iraq collaboration between the British and the monarchy rendered Palace domination over parliament almost complete, except for short periods in 1936 and 1941 when the army briefly gained control. In Jordan under King 'Abdullah, and later under King Hussein, the hold of the Palace over parliament was nearly absolute, except during 1956 when for a short period an alliance was struck between the Palace and the nationalist groups. The first parliamentary elections in Morocco (held in 1963) demonstrated the same pattern of conflict and control; although the Palace coalition (Front for the Defense of Constitutional Institutions) won a lesser number of seats than had been expected, Palace superiority was maintained.

The Palace system of power has usually been upheld by conservative groups committed to the status quo. Opposition has normally consisted of forces ranging from extreme nationalists to Communists. The Palace group itself has usually belonged to the privileged classes—large land-owners, big merchants, the old established families—and political support has come mainly from the urban middle class, the traditionalist elements, the tribal chiefs, and the rural population.

Though the Palace system of power has tended to distort parliamentary procedure and to restrict political freedom, it has not set up absolute rule, as under the patriarchal or the single-party systems of power. It has laid no claim to a final political philosophy; free enterprise and limited government interference have generally characterized its economic orientation.

The strength of the Palace system has derived mainly from two sources: the claim to religious legitimacy on which all Arab monarchies have been grounded, and the fact that the Palace represents a powerful political minority whose fate is indissolubly linked with the monarchical regime. Religious authority is derived by the Hashimites of Jordan (and formerly of Iraq) and the Alawis of Morocco as descendants of the Prophet Muhammad's family, and derived by the Sanussis of Libya and the Sa'udis of Sa'udi Arabia as leaders of Muslim religious orders (the Sanusiyya and Wahhabiyya movements, respectively). The groups most closely linked with the Palace regimes have varied in composition from one country to another. In Hashimite Iraq the Palace group consisted of the old-guard nationalist leaders who had taken part in the Arab revolt of 1916, of representatives of leading Sunni families, and of merchant and middle class moderates; in Jordan of moderate politicians, tribal chiefs, leaders of the Christian and Circassian minorities, and members of the Hashimite family; in Egypt, the Circassian-Turkish aristocracy, and leading members of the large land-owning pasha class; in Morocco, middle class moderate politicians, and leaders of the conservative and religious elements. In Libya the main strength of the monarchy derived from no particular group but rather from the Sanussi order, and the pragmatic fact that the monarchy constituted the best safeguard for Libya's independence and territorial unity.

The main threat to the Palace system of power has always come from the army rather than from parliamentary opposition or political parties. Conversely, the army has been the Palace's principal instrument of political control. In the 1950's upheaval and coup d'état in the Arab world heightened the dependence of the monarchical regimes on their military establishments; the officer corps gained special privileges as well as new status in society. The use of force and extra-legal methods of control increased in all Palace regimes. Although the Palace system in Morocco was able to accommodate a multiparty system by the early 1960's, Palace domination over parliament in Jordan was complete and party freedom greatly restricted.

THE MULTIPARTY SYSTEM OF POWER

Although multiple political parties were formed under the parliamentary monarchical regimes (Iraq and Egypt, Jordan and Morocco), genuine multiparty systems were established only in the republics of Syria and Lebanon, and now and again in Sudan.[13]

Groups and parties had already begun to form around the parliamentary system in both Syria and Lebanon under the mandates. With independence, power became concentrated in two centers: the presidency and parliamentary blocs. In both countries the parliamentary blocs represented feudal and semi-feudal families, the big merchants, and the urban rich. As political parties, they had no firm popular base, nor any clear political doctrine or program; they constituted the so-called "bloc" parties, i.e., parliamentary groups whose principal concern is sectional, group, and individual interest; these are distinguished from "mass" or "doctrinal" parties, which are ideological, national organizations with rigid party discipline aiming at mass recruitment.

In Lebanon, the leading bloc parties in the mid-1960's were the Constitutional party (*al-hizb al-dusturi*), the National bloc (*al-kutla al-wataniyya*), and the Liberal National party (*hizb al-wataniyyin al-ahrar*), which with shifting alliances and fronts had dominated parliament since independence. The establishment of Lebanese political life on the sectarian division of offices and benefits (e.g., the president is to be a Maronite Christian, the prime minister a Sunni Muslim, the Speaker of Parliament a Shi'i Muslim, the minister of defense a Druze, etc.) reinforced the multibloc party system which facilitated the distribution of power among the various interest groups and maintained a balance among the various religious sects. The president of the republic, though limited in his constitutional powers, enjoyed great influence and was able to play a central role in political life as long as he maintained the support of the various political blocs by adhering to the principle of sectarian balance. The first two presidents after independence (Khouri, 1943-1952, Chamoun, 1952-1958) were forced from office, the first for extending his term of office by manipulating a constitutional amendment, and the second for pursuing a policy which disregarded the Christian-Muslim balance and precipitated the civil war of 1958. Despite inefficiency and corruption, the sectarian bloc party system in Lebanon has provided the best guarantee for political stability and for preservation of political as well as economic liberty in the country.

In Syria the National Bloc (*al-kutla al-wataniyya*)—not to be confused with the Lebanese Bloc—grouped together most of the political figures who had carried the brunt of the struggle against the French mandate. It split shortly after independence into two bloc parties, the National party (*al-hizb al-watani*) and the People's party (*hizb al-sha'b*), which, until 1950, dominated parliamentary life in Syria. Since Syria was predominantly Sunni Muslim and therefore free from the sectarian complex prevailing in Lebanon, the bloc system could not last for long. It was destroyed in the early 1950's as the military gradually installed itself in political control and put an end to free party activity. Thereafter, military regimes succeeded one another, but none was able to restore normal political life or to reestablish a genuine multiparty system.

In 1953 Sudan witnessed the beginning of probably the smoothest parliamentary system in the Arab world. The hopes for orderly development of its democratic institutions were strengthened because the political system revolved around two genuinely representative parties, the National Union party (*hizb al-wahda*) and the Nation party (*hizb al-umma*). With no feudal or excessively wealthy class, and no great disparity in social status among the urban Sudanese, political life seemed directed (as in Turkey after the elections of 1950) toward the two-party system. The contest for power followed the strict legalities of the constitution, and demonstrated qualities of moderation and restraint gained by long training under British tutelege. The sudden collapse of parliamentary government in 1958 constituted a serious setback to political development in the Arab world. The military dictatorship dissolved political parties and instituted the pattern of control established in the other Arab "revolutionary" states. It is significant that Sudan was the first country in the Arab world in which military rule was brought down by a popular uprising (1964) and in which civilian rule was restored after many years of army control.

By the mid-1960's only Lebanon and Morocco, in addition to Sudan, had functioning multi-party systems. The relaxation of Palace domination in Jordan, and the gradual development in Libya of the proper political mechanisms could perhaps eventually lead to the development of similar party systems.

THE SINGLE-PARTY SYSTEM OF POWER

The single-party system of power was established in Egypt, Tunisia, Algeria, and Syria. It is characterized by two main features: personalized leadership and monopoly of power by the single party.

By *personalized* leadership is meant that type of leadership which, in addition to exercising the normal powers of office (president, prime minister), also enjoys extra-legal powers derived from the single party and from direct mass support. Gamal 'Abdul-Nasser of Egypt, Habib Bourghiba of Tunisia, Ahmed Ben Bella of Algeria have represented this type of leadership in the Arab world. Although all three leaders held the position of president with clearly defined constitutional powers, they all wielded influence and exercised control far exceeding their constitutional powers. In essence, the functions of office in this system of power are really trappings that strengthen personalized leadership and help give it an aspect of legitimacy.

Personalized leadership need not be a military dictatorship. For example, Kassem's rule in Iraq (1958-1963) constituted a simple military dictatorship because he failed to devise the necessary constitutional bases for his power or to organize a political party that would bestow legitimacy on the exercise of this power; he was forced to fall back on coercion in order to maintain himself in office and was eventually overthrown by a faction in his own army.

Inasmuch as it considers itself the sole source of political truth and guardian of order in society, revolutionary leadership does not allow any kind of political opposition, although the constitution may provide for "right of free political association and expression." There is great similarity here between patriarchal power and single-party rule, both being absolutist in dogma as well as in system of control. The point of difference lies in execution: revolutionary leadership is "rational," choosing specific means to achieve specific ends, whereas patriarchal leadership is "traditional," accepting inherited values and goals and employing customary means to achieve them.

Tunisia, though basically "liberal" in political orientation, nevertheless belongs to the single-party system of power. The Socialist Destour party (as the Neo-Destour was renamed in 1964) exercises the same monopoly over the functions of government as does the Front of National Liberation in neighboring Algeria. Syria and Iraq, after the *Ba'th* party coups on February 7 and March 8, 1963, respectively, introduced a new element into the single-party system by introducing the concept of "collective leadership." This attempt, however, failed as a result of the counter-coup in Iraq (November 18, 1963) and the subsequent dissolution of the Syrian-Iraqi unity scheme. In Iraq a military dictatorship was reestablished under Colonel 'Abdul-Salam Aref, and in Syria the *Ba'th* party reinstituted the same pattern of military control that had existed since the early 1950's.

The military rule established in Sudan under General Ibrahim 'Abboud in 1958 was similar to that set up in Iraq under Kassem in the same year, but it was not accompanied by the bloodshed and violence which characterized the latter. It was neither really revolutionary in social and economic policy nor based on the single-party system of control. Efforts by General 'Abboud to revive constitutional life and to restore a party system proved unsuccessful, a fact which contributed to the developments of October-November 1964 and the fall of military rule.

The strongest feature of the single-party system is that government centralization and a leadership with charismatic appeal have instituted revolutionary social reform and economic development. It is the single-party regime that has come to symbolize the revolutionary wave in the Arab world. Because of it the ideals of social justice, the welfare state, and "socialism" have gained the ascendency in the Arab world in the second half of the twentieth century.

NOTES

1. For a brief survey on the rise of modern Sa'udi Arabia see H. B. Sharabi, *Governments and Politics of the Middle East in the Twentieth Century* (Princeton, N.J., 1962), pp. 225-237.
2. *Ibid.*, pp. 243-254.
3. See H. B. Sharabi, "Libya's Pattern of Growth," *Current History* (January 1963), pp. 41-45.
4. See Elizabeth Monroe, "Kuwayt and Aden: A Contrast in British Policies," *Middle East Journal* (Winter 1964), pp. 63-71.
5. Text of 1946 constitution in Muhammad Khalil, *The Arab States and the Arab League* (Beirut, 1962), I, Doc. 14.
6. Text of Anglo-Egyptian Agreement, 1953, *ibid.*, I, Doc. 74.
7. The Kurdish uprising which broke out in 1962 was not a "national" but a "minority" uprising. A possible exception to the above principle is Sudan, in which the military (national) government was overthrown in 1964 by popular action rather than by coup d'état.
8. See "British Policy in Egypt," J. C. Hurewitz, *Diplomacy of the Near and Middle East* (Princeton, N.J., 1956), II, Doc. 43.
9. See "Treaty of Alliance, July 24, 1922," and "Treaty of Preferential Alliance, June 30, 1930," *ibid.*, II, Docs., 39, 56.
10. Charles F. Gallagher, *The United States and North Africa*

(Cambridge, Mass., 1963), pp. 88-92; also Alal al-Fassi, *The Independence Movements in Arab North Africa,* trans. (Washington, D.C., 1954), pp. 40-78.

11. *Ibid.*, pp. 126-235; also Douglas E. Ashford, *Political Change in Morocco* (Princeton, N.J., 1961), pp. 57-92.

12. See H. B. Sharabi, "Power and Leadership in the Arab World," *Orbis* (Fall 1963), pp. 583-595.

13. See H. B. Sharabi, "Parliamentary Government and Military Autocracy in the Middle East," *Orbis* (Fall 1960), pp. 338-355.

IV. The Decade of the Coups d'État

TO CHANGE A POLITICAL REGIME IMPOSED BY A FOREIGN POWER required a national uprising; to change a political regime under indigenous control needed conspiracy and coup d'état. The decade of coup d'état began with the Syrian coup of 1949 and was completed with the coups in Iraq and Sudan in 1958. During this period every independent country of the Arab East experienced a coup d'état or attempts at a coup d'état. During the same period, the Maghrib carried out its national uprisings against French domination.

Coup d'état succeeded fully in Syria (1949), Egypt (1952), Iraq (1958), Sudan (1958), and Yemen (1962); it failed in Jordan, Sa'udi Arabia, and Lebanon; counter-coups succeeded in Syria (1949, 1951, 1954, 1961, 1963), in Iraq (1963), and failed in Egypt and Sudan. In each country where the coup d'état succeeded it led to the destruction of existing parliamentary institutions and to their replacement by centralized governments under direct or indirect military control.

Why did this method of political seizure become the primary method of political action in the postwar period? Why did the parliamentary system fail to provide for the peaceful struggle for power? Why did political parties fail? Why, in short, did the army enter into politics?

THE DISINTEGRATION OF THE PARLIAMENTARY SYSTEM

There were three principal factors that greatly contributed to the failure of political democracy in the Arab world: (1) the continued existence of foreign domination during the delicate phase in which parliamentary institutions were being established; (2) the monopoly of power by a privileged class; and (3) the exclusion from political responsibility of the younger generation, particularly as it was represented by the doctrinal parties of the 1930's and 1940's.

1. While Britain and France were the means through which Egypt and Iraq, and Syria and Lebanon, acquired parliamentary government, their very presence in these countries violated both the principle and the fact of "democracy" and national sovereignty. French control of Lebanese and Syrian political life made impossible the development of parliamentary habits and institutions, by making a mockery of such practices as peaceful and orderly competition between parties, the formation of responsible political opposition, and free elections. Indeed, in the Syrian and Lebanese elections held between 1927 and 1938, the French authorities inevitably interfered and manipulated the election of only those candidates whom the High Commissioner's office approved. The highest positions of government, including those of president of the republic and cabinet ministers, were filled throughout the mandate by docile pro-French politicians. It is not surprising that the Lebanese and Syrian parliaments turned out to be in most instances debating societies with little effective power or influence on the flow of events.[1]

Britain's interference in the internal political affairs of Egypt and Iraq, though more subtle than the French, had a similarly frustrating influence on the attitudes and habits of those engaged in political life. Although the British never interfered directly in elections, they nevertheless determined, when they so wished, the character and composition of the national governments. Perhaps the most glaring example of Britain's ultimate control over Egyptian political life was the forceful imposition of the Nahas government in 1942.[2] In Iraq, British control was exercised through the various British "advisors" to the government and the army, and through the Hashimite monarchy's conviction that it was unable to survive without British backing; the British ambassador in Baghdad represented the real power behind the throne in Iraq, and was regarded as such by the nationalists.

Parliamentary life, as it was experienced under French and British domination, produced a deep sense of disillusionment, especially in the rising interwar generation; its failure in these countries was attributed not to the circumstances and conditions under which it was established and forced into operation, but to the system itself. Thus involvement in parliamentary elections or in anything related to public office was regarded as a game in which subservience, underhandedness, bribery, and a host of other undesirable qualities were requirements for success.

The distinction between "moderate" and "extremist" acquired new meaning during this phase. Moderation came to signify willingness to serve the status quo and to collaborate with existing power. Many of the old nationalists were drawn into the system and were tainted by association. To the rising generation, parliamentarism came to symbolize the loss of national integrity as much as it did foreign interference and social and economic exploitation. The optimistic vision of nineteenth century liberalism which had inspired the pre-World War I generation was transformed into bitter disappointment after the interwar parliamentary experience. To the younger generation the apparent virility of fascism and socialism exerted great attraction in comparison with the surrounding corruption and inefficiency of parliamentary democracy. Thus neither as a practical political ideal nor as the embodiment of enlightened liberalism was Western-type democracy able to take root in these countries by the time the younger generation was ready to assume political responsibility.

2. The opposition between the older and younger generations of nationalists was by 1945 too bitter and too sharp to allow for mutual accommodation within the established political system.

The old guard nationalists who in 1945 monopolized power in Egypt, Iraq, Syria, and Lebanon had been educated in the old Islamic and Ottoman traditions, in Turkish schools, or abroad in Paris or London, and were mostly either lawyers or (especially in Iraq) former officers of the Ottoman army. As an elite they were simple and unsophisticated in their political views. Their knowledge of Europe did not extend beyond a superficial view of the material progress, power, and parliamentary government. Most of them spoke halting English or French, but they were unequipped to deal substantively with Europeans, and although not all of them spoke Turkish or were educated in Istanbul, they remained "Ottoman" in mentality and disposition. None of their writings have had lasting impact. Most of the old guard belonged to upper class Sunni (in Lebanon also Christian) families; they were polite, hospitable, and charming and in their outlook kind, generous, and aristocratic

But as a group they were disorganized and wholly lacking in discipline.

As the elite of their generation they were the natural leaders of national awakening. After World War I, they provided the slogans of *"istiqlal"* and *"jala'"* (independence and evacuation) and led their followers to their realization. Beyond this point, however, they could not imbue nationalist movements with coherent philosophy or positive political content.

Young and progressive in the 1920's, they were old and conservative by the 1940's; the doctrinal parties of the young restless generation were not within their scope. Their politics during the interwar period were those of the bloc party system, safeguarding sectional interests and protecting the status and wealth of their class. Their system simply could not absorb the doctrinal parties of the younger generation. Denied effective participation in the older generation's exclusive parliamentary system, the young nationalists in Lebanon, Syria, Iraq, and Egypt were finally driven to violence.

3. The new generation which grew to maturity in the 1930's and 1940's was molded by ideas and influences radically different from those to which the older generation had been exposed in its formative years. For one thing, Islam no longer held undisputed sway.

The first doctrinal parties were formed within the growing groups of educated elite in the early 1930's; they were the first political organizations of their kind to emerge in the Arab world. The Muslim Brothers (*al-ikhwan al-muslimun*) was founded in 1927 in Egypt; the *ahali* (People's) group in 1931 in Iraq; the Syrian Nationalist party (*al-hizb al-suri al-qawmi*) in 1932 in Lebanon; the League of National Action (*'usbat al-'amal al-qawmi*) in 1935 in Syria; the Arab Resurrection party (*hizb al-ba'th al-'arabi*) in 1941 in Syria.[3] The Communist party was founded in all these countries during the 1920's but possessed no real strength until the 1940's.

Despite certain fundamental differences in doctrine and goals, all these parties had common characteristics distinguishing them from the political groupings of the older generation. Each had a systematic ideology as the basis of its principles of political and social action and as the justification of its methods and goals; each was hierarchically organized, with a clear-cut center of command and an administrative structure based on the branch or cell type of organization; each aimed at mass recruitment, and instilled its membership with discipline and obedience. The ultimate goal of each of these parties was to gain control of the state to establish a new social and political order. The more they were held off from power, the more opposed they became to the existing system and the more militant. Persecuted by the established regimes and constantly threatened with dissolution, they increasingly resorted to underground organization and the use of violent means. They organized para-military forces, bought and stored weapons, and prepared for the seizure of power by force. The most important step taken by some of these parties was to attempt to mesh their ideological forces with the physical power of the military by infiltration of the army and conversion of younger officers to their views.

THE SEIZURE OF POWER

It is important to remember that all national armies in the Arab world are of recent origin. There exists no military tradition—no military past, no deeply-rooted *esprit de corps,* no traditional officer class. Each has its beginnings in the forces created under foreign domination.[4] Until the end of the Second World War the status of the military was an inferior one; those who volunteered for military service generally belonged to the lower strata of society and only a very few educated young men chose the army for a career.

The postwar period brought a complete transformation in the status of the military throughout the Arab world. With independence the army became a symbol of national pride and dignity, and the military academies of Egypt, Syria, and Iraq were soon crowded with qualified applicants. Within a few years the military establishment had become a center of nationalist activity, with a clear distinction developing between the older and higher-ranking officers identified with the old leadership and the political status quo and the younger junior officers (from the rank of colonel and captain down) opposed to the status quo and, in most instances, affiliated with a revolutionary doctrinal party.

The Palestine War was the first of a series of occasions to bring the army to the fore of political life in the three major states of the Arab Middle East: Egypt, Syria, and Iraq. While the Palestine defeat unmasked the bankruptcy of the old leadership, it also showed that national weakness as well as national power rested in the army. The first Arab army to enter politics was the Syrian, after Col. Husni al-Za'im had executed the first successful coup d'état in the postwar period (March 30, 1949), initiating a pattern which was to dominate Arab political life for the next decade. The ease with which he seized power indicated that the army would henceforth be the principal arbiter in the political struggle for power in the Arab world. Wherever the military did not actually take over during the next decade it nevertheless dominated political development and became, even in the monarchical regimes, a center of influence and prestige.

The coup d'état involves two principal activities, the *seizure* of power and the *maintenance* of power.[5] Given favorable conditions, seizure is relatively easy. The process of seizure in the Arab East may be summarized in five main steps.

First, a "Free Officers" group, usually consisting of junior army officers, lays the foundations of the conspiracy to take over power. The circle of leadership at this stage is small, and of course the identity of its members is secret. Prior to the execution of the coup, the conspiratorial elements are extended and organized into cells both within the army and among civilian political partners. In Egypt the Muslim Brothers constituted the major non-military group with which the Free Officers cooperated. In Syria, the Communists, the Syrian Nationalists (PPS), and the Ba'thists were the main political groups that participated in the secret organizations within the army. In the Iraqi coup of 1958, no civilians were involved.

Recruitment of membership during this organizational stage is on the basis of the candidate's capacity to contribute to the execution of the coup, his political orientation, branch of the service, position of command, political contacts, etc. In Syria, for example, where coups d'état (1949, 1950, 1954, 1961, 1963) had developed into a clear-cut pattern, seizures were successfully carried out by groups that could command the armored units of the Qatana camp (located a few miles west of Damascus), had controlling positions in GHQ, and were able to control the combat units stationed on the Syrian-Israeli front.

The second stage is entered with the decision of when to strike and how. The decision to strike is made within the small circle of leadership. The opportunity presents itself differently under different circumstances. In Egypt, the decision to execute the coup on July 22, 1952, was forced upon the Free Officers by the rapidly deteriorating political situation in the country. In Syria, the first coup of March 30, 1949, was the direct product of the defeat in Palestine and the subsequent paralysis of political leadership in the country. In Iraq, the opportunity to strike presented itself on the night of July 13-14, 1958, when Lt. General Kassem, instead of following army orders to proceed toward Jordan to bolster King Hussein's regime during the crisis of July 1958, moved into Baghdad and carried out the coup d'état. Hesitation has spelled disaster to conspirators in Jordan, Sa'udi Arabia, and Lebanon. Once a conspiracy is afoot it is bound to be uncovered if it does not move swiftly from one step to the next. The actual act of seizure has usually required only a small number of troops. It is important, however, that a sufficient number of tanks and armored cars be available to the conspirators to put down possible resistance and, chiefly, to assist in executing the third step.

The third step consists of securing the positions that are key to the implementation of power: (1) by paralyzing the center of political authority by killing or arresting the leading members of the government; (2) by gaining command of the armed forces through occupation of the ministry of defense (Army GHQ); (3) by disrupting the country's communications network through seizing the centers of communication; (4) by gaining immediate access to the people and the outside world through the central broadcasting station. Failure to achieve any one of these objectives has resulted in the collapse of a coup, e.g., the abortive coup in Lebanon of December 31, 1961, which was prevented from occupying the broadcasting station and the ministry of defense. The two centers of authority, the civilian and the military, are the most immediately important. Failure in these enables large-scale resistance by the government, and the coup d'état is converted into an armed insurrection. Once these centers of authority are taken, all police and administrative organs are automatically crippled.

The fourth step is consolidating power and bringing the country back to normalcy:

(1) Since the first and most important instrument of power is the army, it is the first object of attention. All major commands are assigned to members of the Free Officers group and the command of the army is brought under the direct control of the new leadership. Ranking officers identified with the former regime are immediately arrested, later put on retirement; suspect officers may be dismissed, imprisoned, or sent to remote embassies as military attachés.

(2) Political control and return to normalcy are secured by the setting up of a transitional civilian government composed of old and respected politicians; at the same time, a "Revolutionary Council" of the leaders of the coup d'état forms to wield all the powers of the state.

(3) At this stage, martial law is lifted and normal communication within the country and with the outside world is resumed. The regime's immediate goal is to secure formal recognition of the powers and the important states in the region. As recognition is granted, the new regime may be considered finally established.

The fifth and final step is instituting a new system of political control:

(1) The process of securing trusted army officers and reliable civilian administrators in key positions in government and administration is completed. Internal security is tightened by overhauling the police structure and linking it to army intelligence, which now becomes the principal instrument of internal control. Diplomatic missions are subjected to investigation and major positions are awarded to followers of the new regime.

(2) A period of political transition is declared. The old constitution, first suspended, is formally abrogated, and all political parties are dissolved. The Revolutionary Council which already informally holds all executive and legislative powers, now rules by decree. Restoration of political freedom and constitutional government is promised as soon as the necessary reforms are carried out and the country made ready for "true democracy."

(3) The former regime is discredited by public trials in which the evils committed by its leading members are given wide publicity. At the same time, plans for economic development and social reform are set forth, and promises are made to enlarge and strengthen the country's armed forces. The "hand of friendship"

is extended to all nations that choose to be friendly to the new regime.

THE MAINTENANCE OF POWER

To seize power is one thing, to maintain and preserve it quite another. The most serious threat faced by all regimes created by successful coups d'état is the internal struggle for leadership. At first the collective leadership of the conspiratorial group is carried over into the Revolutionary Council; but as soon as power is established and the Revolutionary Council becomes supreme, dissension arises and the struggle for absolute leadership begins. Every military coup d'état in the Arab world has had the same result: *collective leadership breaks down and is replaced by a dictatorship.*

The establishment of the military dictatorship leads to the first purges of the new regime; their first targets are members of the Revolutionary Council itself. Officers who had opposed the new leadership during the "palace revolution" are now removed, and the supporters of the new leader are promoted to high positions.

At this point, the military dictatorship, based as it is on the usurpation of power, has no institutional foundations of legitimacy. It continues to possess power and to exercise it by virtue of two things: mass support and loyalty of the army.

During the first phase, the military leader enjoys an absolute power which he can exercise without the mediation of political parties and without the institutions and procedures of representative government. As the months pass without miraculous transformations and the drudgery of daily routine returns, enthusiasm invariably begins to subside. In the army, nuclei of resistance begin to form and the conspiratorial process begins again.

To bolster popular support and to maintain firm hold over the army, the military leader must initiate dramatic action (e.g., Nasser's nationalization of the Suez Canal in 1956, Kassem's claim to Kuwait in 1960) and create an atmosphere of danger and tension by occasionally uncovering real or imaginary threats to the regime: "neo-imperialism," "feudalism," "reaction." Internally, he begins to rely more and more on coercion and the machinery of the secret police. Intelligence service becomes increasingly the major prerequisite for political control and large amounts are expended on enlarging its apparatus and expanding its operations (e.g., Col. 'Abdul Hamid Sarraj, head of intelligence in Syria, became the most important man in the country during the Syrian-Egyptian union, 1958-1961).

Neither force nor continuous tension, however, has proved a sufficient safeguard to military dictatorship. Middle Eastern military dictators have worked at establishing a political base to extend political power and at the same time to gain legitimacy. This is why one of Nasser's main objectives in Egypt since 1955 has been to create a political system that would transform his military control into civilian rule—by establishing a single-party regime based on limited national representation: the Liberation Rally (*hay'at al-tahrir*) lasted from 1953 to 1957; the National Union (*al-ittihad al-qawmi*), 1957-1961; and the Arab Socialist Union (*al-ittihad al-'arabi al-ishtiraki*) was created in 1962. Plebiscite became an important means of eliciting popular participation and of giving evidence of national support. The first attempt to create a single-party regime was made by Syria's Adib Shishakli with the creation of the Arab Liberation Movement (*harakat al-tahrir al-'arabi*) in 1953. In Iraq, Kassem endeavored to neutralize political opposition by legalizing several mutually hostile parties in 1961, and at the time of his overthrow (February 8, 1963), he was about to introduce a constitutional framework to serve as the basis of a political system similar to that established by Nasser in Egypt and Shishakli in Syria.

No attempt to "politicise" military rule and to institutionalize dictatorial control has yet eliminated cohesion as a means of control or diminished its highly personalized leadership. Wherever the coup d'état has succeeded, any institutions bearing likeness to a parliamentary system have been destroyed, and representation by plebiscite, elections based on screened candidates, and national bodies limited to "deliberative" powers do not yet provide solutions to the problem of orderly transition of power.

NOTES

1. For the best work in English on the French mandate see Stephen H. Longrigg, *Syria and Lebanon Under the French Mandate* (London, 1958).

2. See Desmond Stewart, *Young Egypt* (London, 1958), p. 116.

3. See Ishak Musa Husaini, *The Moslem Brethren* (Beirut, 1956); Nicola A. Ziyadeh, *Syria and Lebanon* (New York, 1957), 191-200;

Majid Khadduri, *Independent Iraq* (2nd ed., London, 1960), pp. 358-364.

4. For an excellent study of the military in the various countries of the Middle East see Manfred Halpern, *The Politics of Social Change in the Middle East and North Africa* (Princeton, N.J., 1963), pp. 251-280.

5. See H. B. Sharabi, "Parliamentary Government and Military Autocracy in the Middle East," *Orbis* (Fall 1960), pp. 353-355.

V. Socialism and Revolution

"REVOLUTIONARY," "MONARCHICAL," AND "INTERMEDIATE" STATES

The early 1960's witnessed the termination of two parallel developments in the Arab world; in the Arab Middle East the "decade of coup d'état" turned full cycle and a new phase of political consolidation began; in North Africa uprising and revolution reached their logical conclusion and a new pattern of political development set in. The Arab world (except for South Arabia) was now fully independent of foreign domination and fell into three main groups of states. The core group consisted of the four *revolutionary* states of Egypt, Algeria, Syria, and Iraq, which held forth radical social and political reform as principles of progress and upheld the ideologies of Arab nationalism and "socialism." The *monarchical* group was composed of the four antirevolutionary, antisocialist monarchies of Sa'udi Arabia, Jordan, Libya, and Morocco. Lebanon, Kuwait, Yemen, Sudan, and Tunisia constituted an *intermediate* group with varying political structures and economic organization, and different ideological trends.

The first group represented the "revolutionary wave" and constituted the vanguard of the welfare state in the Arab world. The countries of this group differed greatly from one another in their interpretations of "revolution" and "socialism," as well as in the meaning of Arab nationalism and Arab unity, but they were bound together by their repudiation of traditional political and social structures and their stress on basic change in all fields of social and economic endeavor. By the early 1960's they held the initiative in political action within the Arab world; each in its own way represented an experiment in drastic political and economic change.

The four monarchies stood for traditionalism and the preservation of the social and political status quo. They differed from one another in their systems of control and in their social and economic organization, but they were alike in their opposition to all forms of radical change in social or economic life. The main targets of the "revolutionary wave," they were forced to take the defensive in the inter-Arab political struggle.

Between the two extreme positions stood the intermediate states. All five states in this group are to a greater or lesser extent peripheral in a political sense. None had become directly engaged in the power struggle between the "revolutionary" and the "traditionalist" groups, although they often served as the battlefield of this struggle. There were, however, important differences within the group: two, Sudan and Yemen, having undergone military coups d'état, were "revolutionary" in orientation; Kuwait, on the other hand, being a patriarchal shiekhdom, belonged to the traditionalist group; while the westernized republics of Lebanon and Tunisia occupied a middle ground.

Before discussing this structural pattern of Arab political life, it is necessary to outline briefly the rise of the "revolutionary wave" and the establishment of socialist ideology in the four core revolutionary states.

"SOCIALISM" AND THE REVOLUTIONARY STATES

Neither revolution nor socialism had strict theoretical foundations in any of the core countries, but developed pragmatically into various political and economic structures. The ideology of Arab socialism, especially in Egypt and Algeria, seemed to owe more to Proudhon than to Marx, to British socialism than to Communism. The emphasis on social justice and economic reform—which the "revolution" sought to realize through "socialism"—was basically moral in character. In some ways "revolution" and "socialism" really symbolized traditional Islamic social justice.

Genuine application of the socialist revolution began only in the early 1960's when Egypt promulgated the "nationalization decrees" of July 1961. All banks, insurance companies, industries, transportation lines, and hotels were brought under state control, and individual land-holding was reduced to 100 acres. It was the imposition of these decrees as well as the introduction of land reform which gave impetus to the Syrian secessionist movement and broke up the U.A.R. in September 1961; many of these socialist measures were subsequently repealed in Syria and remained so, despite the rise in 1963 of the socialist Ba'th party to power. In Iraq revolutionary socialism in the Egyptian pattern was not introduced until after the split with Syria in November 1963. Large commercial companies as well as banks and insurance companies were nationalized. The program of agricultural reform (*al-islah al-zira'i*), begun after the coup of 1958, was maintained and intensified.

In Algeria the revolution placed socialism on the same level as "the traditional nationalist objective—i.e., independence." The political and administrative structure of the new state was based on the idea of a "purely Algerian socialism" which took the agrarian masses rather than the urban proletariat for its foundation. The vast social and economic upheaval caused by the devastation of the seven-and-a-half-year war, and by the mass exodus of the European settlers made it possible to begin building from the foundations up; thus the nationalization of banks, industries, transport and communications systems, and large land holdings was undertaken in 1963 with a minimum of dislocation or opposition. On the social plane, the basic structures of socialist organization were created along with the administrative and political organs of the state. Under these conditions socialism and revolution were more thoroughly established in Algeria than in any other Arab country.

In their governmental structures and methods of political control the four revolutionary states had more in common than in their social and economic organization. All of them were ultimately based on military control, on personalized leadership, and on the domination of the single party or ruling group. In this respect, Egypt was politically the strongest and internally probably the most stable. The social and religious homogeneity of the Egyptian people, its concentration in 3.5 per cent of the country's land area, and the centuries-old docility of the *fellah,* are all factors that facilitated the establishment of smooth political control and the creation of a monolithic state. Since the coup d'état (1952), constitutional charters had been drafted in 1956, 1958, and 1963, and three legislative bodies elected. The Arab Socialist Union, which replaced the National Union as the single party in the country, served as the basis for the 1964 elections which resulted in a national assembly dominated by peasants and members of the working class. As an Arab "socialist republic," Egypt had the strongest military establishment in the Arab world, and was from the standpoint of the world powers the most important Arab state. The success of the Egyptian revolution and Egypt's position of leadership in Arab and African affairs is in great part attributable to the dynamic leadership of Gamal 'Abdul-Nasser, who despite his decline as a pan-Arab leader remained the leading figure in the Arab world.

When Algeria achieved independence in July 1962, more than half of its population had been uprooted—one million killed, two million homeless, and nearly four million living on aid and governmental subsidies. The political system established by the end of 1963 was based on the Front of National Liberation (FLN) and the Algerian National Army (ANA). The constitution promulgated in September 1963 consolidated the single party regime and gave the FLN total monopoly over the political processes of the country, including the government, elections, and the national assembly. The president of the party's Political Bureau, Ahmed Ben Bella, became the president of the republic, and the army was given control in the government by the appointment of its commander-in-chief, Col. Houari Boumedienne, as vice-president, and by the appointment of several army officers to high executive positions. As in Egypt, an assembly was elected and parliamentary government was introduced, but all effective power rested with the executive. By early 1964 almost all the former leaders of the revolution had resigned, been removed from power, or had dissociated themselves from Ben Bella's regime, which was now menaced by opposition from the bourgeois moderates and extreme socialists alike, but was backed by the mass of the population. The coup d'état which removed Ben Bella from power in June 1965 served to entrench the army more firmly in the country's political life.

Neither Iraq nor Syria had the internal strength or political coherence which Egypt and Algeria possessed. Neither was able to evolve a system in which military rule could be sufficiently politicized to introduce some form of permanence and stability to the regime. The legal vacuum created by the successive coups and counter-coups made it increasingly difficult in either country to restore political balance or to establish a new system of political organization. In this sense, the socialist revolution cannot be said to have altogether succeeded in Syria and Iraq, though the political revolution did; in both countries preoccupation with the problem

POLITICAL STRUCTURE (1965)

Country	Form of Government	Constitution Promulgated	Political System	Executive	Coup d'État	Chief of State
Morocco[1]	Monarchy	1963	Multiparty	Palace (Cabinet)	(attempted) 1963	Hasan II
Algeria[2]	Republic	1963	Single-party	President	None	Boumedienne
Tunisia[3]	Republic	1959	Single-party	President	(attempted) 1962	Bourghiba
Libya[1]	Monarchy	1951	Political oligarchy	Palace (Cabinet)	None	Idris I
Egypt[2]	Republic	1964	Single-party	President	1952	'Abdul-Nasser
Sudan[3]	Republic	1956 (Transitional const.)	Multiparty	President	1958	. . . .
Lebanon[3]	Republic	1926	Multiparty	President	(attempted) 1961	Helou
Syria[2]	Republic	1964 (Provisional const.)	Single-party	Premier/Revolutionary Council	(last) 1963	Hafiz
Jordan[1]	Monarchy	1952	Multiparty (nonoperational)	Palace (Cabinet)	(attempted several times) 1956-1962	Hussein I
Iraq[2]	Republic	1964 (Provisional const.)	Military hegemony	President	(last) 1963	'Aref
Kuwait[3]	Sheikhdom (Monarchical)	1962	Geschlecterstaat	Palace (Cabinet)	None	Al-Sabah
Sa'udi Arabia[1]	Monarchy	None	Geschlecterstaat	Palace (Cabinet)	(attempted) 1958-1959	Feisal
Yemen[3]	Republic	1964 (Provisional const.)	Military hegemony	President	(last) 1962	Sallal

(1) "Monarchical" state. (2) "Revolutionary" state. (3) "Intermediate" state.

of maintaining power retarded economic development and the systematic application of socialist reform principles. Whereas the army in Egypt and Algeria had been incorporated into the system of government and domination canalized through the administrative and political structures of the state, in Syria and Iraq military control remained supreme and continued to be exercised more or less directly.

THE REVOLUTIONARY WAVE

The revolution, once successfully established in the core revolutionary states, especially in Egypt and Algeria, could not be confined within the borders of these states. Indeed, the validity of revolutionary theory was to be established precisely by its extension to the surrounding countries. The first slogans of the revolutionary offensive waged by Egypt and Syria beginning with the mid-1950's merely called for the overthrow of corrupt government and the establishment of social justice. Later, with Nasser's adoption of the ideology of Arab nationalism, the driving force of the revolutionary momentum became Arab unity.[1] Until the emergence of independent Algeria in 1962, Egypt was the unquestioned leader and spokesman of the new Arab revolution, which under the name of "Nasserism" (*al-nassiriyya*) had created a wide following throughout the Arab world. An important factor for the stability of Nasser's rule in Egypt and his rise to international prominence was his acknowledged leadership of the "Arab revolution."

Kassem's reluctance to join, and later his opposition to Egyptian-led Arab nationalism, constituted the first major setback to the movement of Arab unity and greatly contributed to the collapse in 1961 of the Syrian-Egyptian union. It was only after Syria's cession from the UAR that the Egyptian leadership introduced the new element of "Arab socialism" (*al-ishtirakiyya al-'arabiyya*) into revolutionary ideology.[2] Unity among the various Arab states was now seen as insufficient or even impossible unless preceded by the socialist revolution. Thus the fundamental tenet of Arab nationalism—the unification of all the Arab states from the Atlantic Ocean to the Persian Gulf—lost its primacy and became conditional upon the success of the "socialist" revolution in each Arab state. This shift was signaled by 'Abdul-Nasser's dissolution of the "National Union," the party that upheld nationalist revolutionary ideology, and the establishment (December 1962) of the "Arab Socialist Union."

The new socialist tendency in the Arab world was further strengthened by the success of the extremist wing of the Algerian revolution and the emergence in 1962 of Ben Bella as the leader of the FLN and the declaration of a "socialist democratic state" in an independent Algeria under his leadership. The close resemblance in political structure (single-party, presidential constitutional framework, personalized leadership) and ideological orientation (socialism) between Egypt and Algeria brought the two countries closer together and made them the springboard of revolutionary socialist ideology in the Arab world.

THE MONARCHICAL REGIMES AND THE REVOLUTIONARY WAVE

In terms of inter-Arab politics it was natural that the states to have been most exposed to the impact of the revolutionary wave, and most threatened by it, were the monarchies—Sa'udi Arabia, Yemen, Libya, Jordan, and Morocco. They were the "reactionary" states which stood for the "old order," "class privilege," and "feudalism," and they obstructed the establishment of the "just socialist order."

The two traditionalist monarchies, Sa'udi Arabia and Libya, were the least prepared of the four monarchies to cope with the challenge of revolution.

Sa'udi internal control was tightened in the early 1960's under the leadership of Prince Faisal, then Crown Prince, who introduced rigorous financial and administrative reforms into the machinery of the state. In 1964 Faisal assumed full control of the government, and was officially proclaimed King in November of the same year. The army, not more than 10,000 men, was kept small and dispersed throughout the kingdom. Demands to enact a constitution were opposed by Faisal, who instead strengthened governmental control and prohibited any form of political activity. Though Sa'udi Arabia had a strong government apparatus and a functioning administrative bureaucracy, its future as a state seemed uncertain and depended primarily on the person of the king and on the continued solidarity of the Sa'udi princes.

In Libya the monarchical regime was threatened for other

reasons—mainly because Crown Prince Muhammad al-Rida, the King's cousin, appeared incapable of maintaining the supremacy of the monarchy or of preserving the unity of the country. Ever since independence Libya had tried to be neutral in Arab politics and to maintain friendly relations with all states, conservative and revolutionary alike. This policy of nonalignment was accelerated following the discovery of oil in 1959, and internal conservatism was strengthened. Political parties, formed in the early 1950's, were soon dissolved and the activities of the budding workers' movement greatly restricted. To further prevent the spread of revolutionary ideas, severe measures were taken to curb the influx of workers and technicians from other Arab countries, especially Palestinians and Egyptians, the most passionate supporters of Nasserism and vocal advocates of the revolution and socialism. Non-Libyan Arabs already working in Libya were subjected to stringent controls, and many of them, including large numbers of Egyptian teachers, were forced to leave the country under one pretext or another.

Jordan and Morocco confronted the revolutionary wave with dynamic action, mostly because of the energy and resilience of their two young kings, Hussein of Jordan and Hassan of Morocco. King Hussein, who ascended the throne in 1953 at the age of eighteen, weathered repeated attempts to overthrow the monarchical regime and actively counteracted the propaganda attacks and subversive activity of Syria and Egypt. He reacted to domestic political opposition by the dissolution of all political parties in 1957 and by establishing a military rule which he himself directed. The civil administration was subjected to periodic purges of suspected elements, and parliament was reduced to a rubber stamp. By maintaining his power over the army, Hussein succeeded not only in preserving the monarchy but in bestowing on his regime a stability which the neighboring revolutionary states of Syria and Iraq lacked; in 1964, after the Arab summit conference in Cairo, he emerged a leading figure in Arab politics, giving the monarchical camp new vigor and vitality.

Hassan of Morocco ascended the throne in 1961 and immediately took command of political life. As his father before him, he was aware of the fact that for the monarchy to survive, the King himself must remain at the center of political life in the country. The two traditional bases of the Moroccan monarchy were the army and the conservative elements of the population, and these Hassan now cultivated with energy. Unlike Hussein of Jordan, he allowed a great measure of political activity, playing one party against the other. He was able further to strengthen his position by introducing in 1963 the first constitution in Moroccan history.[3]

Under the constitution, Morocco had one of the only three multiparty systems in the Arab world. The Palace was represented by the *Front pour la défense des institutions constitutionelles* (FDIC), which together with the *Mouvement Populaire* (representing the Berber tribes) and a group of conservative liberals, came to form the Democratic Socialist party (1964) which backed the monarchy. The other two major parties were the conservative bourgeois *Istiqlal,* and the leftist, antimonarchical *Union national des forces populaires* (UNFP), which had split from the *Istiqlal* in 1959 under the leadership of Mehdi Ben Barka and a group of young socialist intellectuals. A new political force was represented by Morocco's two labor unions, *Union Marocaine du Travail* (UMT), which leaned toward the UNFP, and the *Istiqlal*-oriented *Union Général des Travailleurs Marocains* (UGTM). In the 1963 referendum, the *Istiqlal* backed the constitution and on the whole supported the monarchy; the UNFP, on the other hand, opposed the constitution and in the parliamentary elections of 1963 ran against the Palace groups. The UNFP represented the force of revolution in Morocco and enjoyed the backing of Algeria and Egypt. The first parliamentary elections (May 1963) gave the Palace front only 69 seats, the *Istiqlal* 43, the UNFP 28, and independents four.[4]

THE INTERMEDIATE STATES AND THE REVOLUTIONARY WAVE

All five intermediate states—Lebanon, Tunisia, Kuwait, Yemen, Sudan—were at one time or other the target of subversive action by one or more of the core revolutionary states. Egyptian support of the anti-Bourghiba faction led by Salih Ben Yousef resulted in an armed insurrection in 1955, nearly precipitating civil war in Tunisia; Egypt persisted until 1956 in trying to pull Sudan into a larger "Nile Valley"; Syrian-Egyptian subversion in Lebanon led to the Lebanese civil war of 1958; Iraq in 1961 laid claim to Kuwait as part of Iraqi national territory; Egyptian attacks on the Yemeni King, Imam Ahmad, led to the Egyptian supported military coup d'état of 1962, bringing about prolonged civil war in Yemen.

Each of these states made adjustments in internal organization and adopted regional and foreign policies to shield itself against external interference, subversion, or attack. Sudan and Yemen, owing to successful coups d'état (1958 and 1962, respectively), fell within the fold of the "revolutionary" states. They both upheld republicanism and paid lip service to principles of Arab unity and socialism; following Egypt's example, they adopted policies of nonalignment and accepted aid from both East and West.

Kuwait followed two courses of action to ward off revolution. In 1962 it introduced radical political reforms, which based the patriarchal system, at least in theory, on constitutional structures and set up an "Arab Development Fund" through which it channeled a portion of its oil revenues into the other Arab states.[5] In its regional policy, Kuwait courted the revolutionary states, especially Egypt, and at the same time maintained correct relations with the monarchical regimes. Its foreign policy was anchored on friendship with Great Britain, the bulwark and guardian of Kuwait's continued independence.

The two most important states of the intermediate group are Lebanon and Tunisia. They are peripheral in the political sense—in their attempts to remain outside the main stream of Arab political life—but central in their importance to the cultural and intellectual development of the Arab world. Despite differences in social composition and political and economic organization, they have much in common. They are among the smallest states of the Arab world (except for Kuwait they have the smallest population and territory); they are both Mediterranean in culture and orientation; each has its back to the desert and faces Europe openly; and they are both inclined to be pro-Western despite their formal positions of neutrality.

Lebanon's 1958 civil war affected its political life more profoundly than the experience of Ben Yousef's rebellion did Tunisia's in 1955. Lebanese neutrality had been violated during the Chamoun administration (1952-1958), which actively opposed

Nasserism and openly followed a pro-Western, and particularly pro-American, policy. It disrupted the internal balance between Muslims, who were generally pro-Nasser, and Christians, who were generally in favor of close relations with the West, making civil war inescapable—especially in view of massive UAR support to the pro-Nasserite groups. The civil war cost many hundred dead and almost brought about the collapse of the Lebanese economy. United States intervention led to the cessation of hostilities, the restoration of the sectarian balance by the neutralization of the warring factions, and halted UAR intervention. Though the army did not seize the opportunity given to it to take over power, it now gained political ascendancy, and its commander-in-chief, General Fu'ad Shehab, was elected president of the republic. The "national pact" was reinstated and the country gradually returned to normalcy. Parliamentary elections took place in 1960 and again in 1964, and a precarious democratic regime was maintained, based on the sectarian balance and the good will of the army. So long as equilibrium between Muslim and Christian was preserved, and the revolutionary states (principally Syria and Egypt) refrained from backing one group against another, and the economic boom continued, Lebanese political independence appeared secure.

Just as Lebanon lay in the zone of UAR activity, Tunisia was exposed to Egyptian influence and, after 1962, to that of Algeria as well. Tunisia's pro-Western orientation became a prime target of revolutionary propaganda, but its internal cohesion and political resilience enabled it to withstand external pressure. Tunisia's political system derived its strength from sources quite different from those underpinning the Lebanese system.[6] The social and religious homogeneity of the Tunisian people, and the genuine representation which the country's single-party system was able to provide, imbued its political structure with remarkable solidarity and strength. Unlike any other party in the Arab world, the Neo-Destour (Destour Socialist party), backed by the Tunisian labor organization, dominated political life but did not provide the grounds for a full-fledged dictatorship. In its orientation and the social composition of its membership, the party faithfully reflected the country's dominant elements—the conservative rural masses, the French-educated bourgeoisie, and the leftist intellectuals. The party itself was organized in the European fashion, divided into regional federations headed by elected committees, and a central Political Committee composed of ten elected members, with a chairman who was also the president of the party. As in Turkey under Mustafa Kemal, the president of the party—Habib Bourghiba—was also president of the republic, and its leading officers constituted the core of governmental hierarchy and dominated parliament. Tunisia, like Lebanon, strove not to alienate its powerful neighbors; it paid lip service to Arab nationalism and Arab unity and gave full backing to the concept of Maghribi unity. Its main concern, however, was to consolidate its own independence and preserve its political system and economic organization.

What softened the brunt of the revolutionary assault on the monarchical regimes and the peripheral states alike was the lack of a united front among the four core revolutionary states. Indeed, Egypt's attempts to dominate the other three centers of the revolution—Damascus, Baghdad, and Algiers—had had a divisive effect on the revolutionary front. The rise in 1963 of the Ba'th in Damascus and Baghdad threatened Egypt's leadership, and in large part explains Nasser's refusal to enter into unity discussions with Syria and Iraq so long as the Ba'th held exclusive power in the two countries. This in turn led to the disintegration of Ba'thist ascendancy in Iraq and the breakdown of the Syrian-Iraqi front. In North Africa, Egypt backed Ben Bella's Algerian revolutionary regime and succeeded in attracting a strong ally. But the dominance which Egypt exercised in Syria during the Syrian-Egyptian union and in Yemen after the 1962 coup could not be asserted in Algeria. The Algerian revolution considered itself the *avant garde* movement in the Arab world and Africa, and as such sought to establish its own position of leadership and pursue its own independent revolutionary policies.[7] To the Algerians Arab nationalism did not constitute, as it did for the Eastern Arabs, the driving force in the revolution, and the goal of Arab unity seemed a remote and rather unattainable aspiration. What bound Egypt and Algeria together were the broader revolutionary goals—common opposition to traditionalist regimes, and adherence to nonalignment in the world conflict. In this they were joined in principle by Syria and Iraq and followed by Yemen and Sudan. The continued state of flux, however, which characterized the Arab world in the mid-

1960's precluded either permanent alliances or lasting enmities. The phenomenon of revolution alone was the constant and prevailing force of political life.

THE REVOLUTIONARY STATES AND THE COLD WAR

The boldest and most systematic policies of the revolutionary states were in the field of foreign policy.

The Bandung conference of 1955, joining all the former colonial countries in a new power bloc, marked the beginning of the reorientation of the revolutionary states of the Arab world in the cold war. Until roughly the mid-1950's the Middle East and North Africa had been exclusively a Western preserve. The first country to commit itself to an agreement with the Communist bloc was Egypt, when in September 1955 an arms deal was concluded with Russia via Czechoslovakia. The nationalization of the Suez Canal Company in July 1956, following the withdrawal of offers of Western aid for the Aswan Dam, constituted a second blow to Western influence, from which it has not fully recovered. The 1956 invasion of Suez by Britain, France, and Israel put the Soviet Union and the United States on the same side and brought about the evacuation of Egyptian territory under joint American-Soviet pressure.

Two major consequences resulted from these developments. First, Egypt demonstrated that in the post-colonial world national sovereignty can be fully exercised by smaller nations against former colonial powers; and second, that since full sovereignty could be exercised, the smaller nations need not be committed either to East or to West. Egypt assumed the position of "positive neutrality," joining India and Yugoslavia, and was followed first by the revolutionary states, and later by the rest of the Arab countries.

This in effect eliminated Western supremacy in the Arab world and established a balance between the Soviet Union and the United States, neutralizing the area. The Eisenhower Doctrine of 1957, which aimed at safeguarding the West's position by bolstering the 1955 Baghdad Pact,[8] proved ineffective. In 1957 Syria, with Egyptian backing, concluded an agreement with the Soviet Union for economic and military assistance, and in 1958 and 1959 Iraq and Yemen followed suit. American Secretary of State Dulles' last efforts were to isolate Egypt and curb the spread of the revolutionary wave by creating a monarchical center of leadership through support of Sa'udi Arabia and Jordan. This clearly came to naught when Egypt united with Syria in 1958, and Iraq, following the coup in July of that year, joined the revolutionary core and in 1959 withdrew from the Baghdad Pact.

In the 1960's the Soviet Union was building the Aswan Dam in Egypt and giving military assistance to Egypt, Syria, Iraq, Yemen, Morocco, and Sudan. In Algeria the Soviet Union, Communist China, Yugoslavia, and Cuba, who had given substantial aid to the revolution, were treated as the strongest allies of the Algerian people. Tunisia and Jordan, who had maintained hostile attitudes toward the Communist bloc (despite their official policies of nonalignment), had established diplomatic relations with the Soviet Union and accepted Communist aid.

By 1961 the right of the Arab countries to exercise neutral policies had been implicitly acknowledged by the United States, and principles of radical social and economic change had been accepted. The United States' primary objective was to maintain stability and balance among the various states of the area. In the Arab-Israeli problem, the most explosive of Middle Eastern problems, the United States continued to play the role of referee and concentrated its efforts on preventing the resumption of hostilities between the two camps. But in the final analysis the United States' commitment to the preservation of the state of Israel limited its ability to back revolutionary Arab nationalism to the extent to which both the Soviet Union and Communist China were able and prepared to back it.

NOTES

1. See H. B. Sharabi, "The Egyptian Revolution," *Current History* (April 1962), pp. 233-241.
2. Malcolm Kerr, "The Emergence of a Socialist Ideology in Egypt," *Middle East Journal* (Spring 1962), pp. 127-144.
3. *The Constitution of the Kingdom of Morocco,* English trans., Embassy of Morocco, Washington, D.C.
4. See Stuart Schaar, "King Hassan's Alternatives," *Africa Report* (August 1963), pp. 7-12.
5. See Fakhri Shehab "Kuwait: A Super-Affluent Society," *Foreign Affairs* (April 1964), p. 474.

6. For text of Tunisian Constitution see Muhammad Khalil, *The Arab States and the Arab League* (Beirut, 1962), I, pp. 449-456.

7. For text of Algerian Constitution see *Middle East Journal* (Summer 1963), pp. 446-450.

8. Text in Hurewitz, *ibid.*, II, Doc. 108.

VI. Revolutionary Ideology

THE NEW LEFT

The postwar revolutionary wave—or as it became known in the Arab world, revolutionism (*al-thawriyyah*)—developed only partly as a reaction to European domination; it was also a natural growth of the revolutionary ideas disseminated by the doctrinal parties founded in the late 1930's and in the 1940's. *Al-thawriyyah,* in this sense, is not just a political revolution, but represents a comprehensive attitude toward social and economic life, including new values and criteria of thought.

While the doctrinal parties of the thirties and forties had emphasized political theory, the revolution emphasized socialism and social justice as the goals of political action. All postwar revolutionary regimes have adhered to socialist programs which, though differing in structure and content from country to country, are basically the same in tone and orientation. The crux of the new trend was a common conviction implicit in revolutionism: that social justice could not be achieved without radically changing two basic elements in Arab society, the prevailing system of ownership and the existing class structure. This is why the concept of the welfare state has—in Egypt, Algeria, Syria—gained a militant character, and revolutionary leadership a moral claim.

The formulation of a socialist doctrine was a gradual and in great part a pragmatic process. The awakening of moral conscience in the postwar intelligentsia provided the groundwork for this development. Islamic social morality compounded with nationalist fervor acted as the emotional propeller of the new doctrine, a fact which in great part accounts for the non-Marxist character of Arab socialism and its hostility to Communism.

Revolutionary socialism has repudiated parliamentary democracy, whose ideology had been imported from Europe and whose institutions were introduced during the period of European domination. The principle of popular democracy, however, was not relinquished. *Genuine* democracy was now seen to consist not in individual freedom protected by traditional parliamentary structures, but rather in social and economic liberation, the bases of true political equality. In order to establish social and economic justice it was considered essential first to reform the social order, then to build a revolutionary economy. The rapid accomplishment of this necessitated the establishment of the single-party regime and the state as the repository of total power. The failure of bourgeois liberalism in the Arab world must be viewed as not so much the failure of the system of liberal democracy itself but rather of the values which had animated this system in the Arab countries. Arab "leftist" thought is a rebellion against a social injustice which in many respects resembled the rebellion of the ideological and socialist revolutionaries in early nineteenth century Europe. In this light, oppression is the perpetuation of the social and economic systems created under European domination and represents an extension of European capitalist exploitation. Independence, therefore, to become meaningful, must first bring about the economic and social liberation of the masses and, as a second step, their integration into the political order of society.

In this respect the crystalization of the postwar intelligentsia's attitude toward Europe afforded, if not a systematic ideology, at least a starting point from which a new social and political outlook could gradually be formulated. Though part of the contemporary elite has maintained its allegiance to the fundamental principles of the European cultural tradition, the ascendency has been seized by the revolutionary, antibourgeois left. In the eyes of the leftist intelligentsia the liberal intellectuals not only retained elements of "decadent intellectualism" but also constituted the articulate bulwark of the antirevolutionary forces, and as such were the ally of reaction and imperialism in the Arab world.

FEATURES OF THE NEW IDEOLOGY

Perhaps the most significant fact about Arab revolutionism is that it is no longer proclaimed by parties still struggling to gain recognition and power, but by established regimes in full control of the state. Revolutionism was for the first time given official formulation by the Front of National Liberation in Algeria, the

Arab Socialist Union in Egypt, and the Socialist Arab Ba'th party in Syria.

(1) The Algerian social and economic program, which was adopted by the Algerian National Revolutionary Council meeting in Tripoli, Libya, on May 27, 1962, outlined in full detail the ideological bases of the FLN and provided the groundwork for the Algerian constitution which was promulgated the following year.[1] (2) The Pact of National Action for Egypt was presented to the National Congress of Popular Forces and unanimously approved, after analysis and discussion, on June 30, 1962,[2] giving the official definition of "Arab Socialism" and providing, like the Algerian program, the theoretical and ideological bases of the Egyptian constitution promulgated two years later. (3) The "Ideological Starting Points" of the Ba'th party, which were adopted at the Sixth Congress of the party's national council on October 28, 1963 (consisting of representatives from various Arab countries but dominated by Syrians), represented the first full statement of Ba'th socialist ideology and the party's political program.[3]

Despite differences in organization and in certain theoretical details, all three programs contained basically the same ideas, expressed in more or less the same terminology. Revolution is the only road to genuine social and economic reform. The base of the revolution consists of the "popular masses" (*al-jamahir al-sha'biyya*), composed of the two principal classes, the peasants and the workers. The vanguard consists of the "revolutionary intellectuals," deriving from the "small bourgeoisie" and professional classes. The conservative elements—the large landowners, big merchants, the old feudal oligarchies—constitute the forces of reaction and the allies of capitalist imperialism; as such they are excluded from participation in the revolutionary effort. The socialist order is to be based on state control, but private ownership is not abolished. Nationalization of large land-holdings, industries, banks, and public utilities is viewed as the natural procedure for bringing down the old bourgeois structures and establishing the socialist order. The agrarian revolution is defined as fundamental to all social and economic change.

In the Egyptian "National Pact," the links with Islam are emphasized as providing "guides to justice and righteousness"; the Ba'th program ignores Islam altogether. The FLN, on the other hand, stresses both Islam and Arabism, but at the same time warns against "those who . . . use Islam for demagogic purposes and to evade facing up to the real issues," and implicitly relegates Islam to the "educational and personal" realms of endeavor.

In their analysis of the state, neither the Egyptian nor the Algerian pronouncements make any direct reference to the nature and character of revolutionary leadership, while the Ba'th program devotes a special section to it. Under "Organizational Problems of the Party and its Relation to the Masses and the Seat of Power," stress is put on two cardinal points: the primacy of "collective leadership" as against the leadership by the single person, and the necessity to draw clear distinction between party leadership and government, underlining the two different areas of power.

The principle of revolutionary democracy is upheld by all three positions. In the Egyptian Pact democracy is simply defined as an "extension of revolutionary action."

> Nobody can be regarded as free to vote without three guarantees: freedom from exploitation in all its forms; equal opportunity for a fair share of the national wealth; and freedom from all anxiety concerning future security.[4]

The Ba'th and the FLN underscore the distinction between "socialist" democracy and Western-type "capitalistic" democracy and stress the "popular" character of democracy. Significantly, they both use the term "people's democracy."

All three revolutionary positions affirm centralization of power and adhere without reservation to the single-party system. They also uphold the principle of national representation based on integration of the masses into the system of power. In this the Egyptian Pact goes perhaps farthest in stipulating that "peasants and workers must fill half the seats in political and popular organizations at all levels—including the Representative Assembly." [5] In the same vein the FLN holds that the goals of the revolution can be achieved only by the people—"by the 'people' we mean peasants, workers, tenants, and revolutionary intellectuals." [6] The Ba'th bases the entire political structure of both the party and the state on peasants and workers: "the socialist revolution is bound to [have] the peasants and the workers as the backbone and base of both the revolution and the party." [7]

The opposition between the revolutionary wave and the forces of reaction is emphasized in all three programs. The polarity between the "progressive revolutionary elements" and the "reactionary and opportunistic" forces (supported by "imperialism and colonialism") operates not only in each country but throughout the Arab world, making for a clear differentiation between two warring camps, one of revolution and progress, the other of reaction and conservatism. Extending the revolution into the "nonliberated" countries of the Arab world is implicitly recognized by the Algerian and Egyptian ideologists as the mission of the revolutionary states; it is explicitly expressed by the Ba'th party which proclaims its goal of carrying the revolution into the other Arab states until "the unitary socialist revolution triumphs throughout the Arab fatherland." [8]

Likewise, there is general agreement among the three revolutionary positions regarding Arab unity, which is set up as an essential objective of revolutionism. As to the mode of its achievement, however, there is not the same agreement. The Ba'th sets up unity as an immediate and primary objective that should be achieved simultaneously with the establishment of the socialist order; and, keeping the failure of the Syrian-Egyptian union in mind, it stipulates that unity should be "on the basis of regional equality and collective leadership," not on that of the ascendency of one country over another.[9] The Egyptian Pact, mindful of the same experience, declares that unity "cannot be imposed," [10] but at the same time makes it clear that Egypt would support all movements striving for unity "without hesitating over the outworn argument of interference in the affairs of others." [11] The Pact also precludes cooperation with other political parties on the grounds that the movement for unity in each country must be the expression of a "national front" combining all parties, not that of a particular party; hence, "the UAR must be careful not to involve itself in the local party disputes of any Arab state and must place the call for unity at the highest level. . . ." [12] The FLN, though stressing the need for unity, sets up Arab unity on a par with Maghribi and African unity: "The major task of our party is to help in assessing the requirements for establishing unity in the Maghrib, in the Arab world, and in Africa. . . ." [13]

With regard to the East-West struggle there is close agreement on positive neutrality, nonalignment, disarmament, prohibition of nuclear testing, and opposition to imperialism. The FLN and the Ba'th underline the special links binding the revolutionary Arab countries with the "socialist countries of the World." The Ba'th expresses this emphatically: "It is to be emphasized that the policy of nonalignment should not prevent us from strengthening the ties of friendship with all the peoples of the socialist world." [14]

POLITICAL BEHAVIOR AND REVOLUTIONISM

Power, once seized, tends to set its own laws and create its own needs. Ideologies and political forms in large part come to reflect the psychological and political environment that comes into being with the seizure of power and the emergence of a new pattern of control in society. Perhaps the most significant feature of power under those conditions is that the structures on which it establishes itself remain contingent upon the return of daily routine and established habits and patterns of behavior.

In none of the revolutionary states of the Arab world have institutional structures and the daily routine of government been established to the point of insuring total legitimacy of revolutionary power or of guaranteeing the smooth and uninterrupted development and growth of revolutionary orders. Stabilization of power, however, particularly in Egypt and Algeria, has progressed sufficiently to create firm footholds for the revolution. In Syria, on the other hand, when the revolutionary process reached its maximum force, the revolution failed to establish sound foundations based on popular backing and was incapable of acquiring lasting legitimacy. In Iraq, internal conflict and the constant threat of counter-coup, has, as in Syria, blocked genuine stability and maintained the initial tension of revolution, a fact which has prevented the creation of those conditions that would allow for the return of routine and established institutional life.

Though revolutionism has failed to win all the states of the Arab world, it has nevertheless succeeded in transforming political environment and in creating new patterns and values in Arab political behavior. To summarize the main features of the revolution, let us briefly consider the following ten points:

1. *Integration of the Masses*. Perhaps the most lasting impact of the revolution has been the awakening of moral consciousness

in Arab political life. This means the recognition by all governments in the Arab world of the social and economic rights of the common man. The sense of obligation to the masses evoked by the "socialism" of the revolutionary states has reflected itself in both the sweeping revolutionary reforms of the core states and in the political and economic measures taken by the other Arab states, including the most traditional, to improve the lot of the common man. For the first time in Arab history the common man has been integrated into the body social and given the opportunity to play an increasingly important role in economic and political life.

2. *New Leadership.* The revolution has created a new type of leadership in the Arab world—dedicated, austere, audacious. To hold office came to mean public service, not personal profit and self-aggrandizement. Centralized rule proved its capacity for quick decision and effective action. The ideal of the benevolent dictator gained strength to such an extent that a new kind of legitimacy has come to be associated with it; the self-indulgence and corruption of the old type of leadership appears in perspective petty and traitorous. The new standards of conduct set by such men as Nasser and Ben Bella have forced even such a traditionalist absolutist monarchy as Sa'udi Arabia to undertake severe corrective measures to maintain a modicum of respect in the eyes of its people.

3. *International Position.* The revolution not only put an end to the last vestiges of foreign domination, but also forced the great powers to deal with the Arab states on a footing of equality and respect. For the first time since Napoleon's invasion of Egypt, a genuine autonomy was achieved in the Arab world that made it possible fully to exercise true national sovereignty. This elimination of Western influence finally allowed the Arab states to pursue independent policies of neutrality and nonalignment.

4. *Authoritarian Rule.* The destruction of the old ruling classes and elimination of parliamentary procedures and the multiparty system prepared the ground for a new kind of authoritarianism in the Arab world. Authoritarian government, not confined to the dictatorships created by revolutionary action, has been established throughout the Arab world. In republican Tunisia, for example, Bourghiba's power is limited only by the structure of the Neo-

Destour party and by the political sophistication of the ruling Tunisian elite; in terms of political structure and system of control, however, Tunisia has all the conditions of a centralized, dictatorial government. In the monarchical regimes, supremacy lies—regardless of the prevailing pattern of political life—in the "palace." Concentration of power, ascendancy of the state, and the predominance of governmental control have become natural attributes of political life in all Arab countries under the impact of revolutionary ideology and pattern of control.

5. *Monopoly of Political Truth.* The core revolutionary states have laid claim to exclusive possession of political truth in society. No opposition to the established order is tolerated, not merely because this would reestablish the inefficiency and corruption of the old multiparty system, but primarily because the revolution claims to have the final solution to all the political and social problems of society.

6. *Social Stratification.* The revolution has destroyed the upper ruling class and given form and status to the lower classes of society. But it has created another kind of social stratification. On top a new ruling class has come into being, composed of the small leadership circle and the higher-ranking army officers and government officials. Situated between the masses and the ruling class, a new kind of "middle class" has emerged, rooted neither in economic nor social grounds, but deriving its character from its functions in the new social order. To this class belongs the lower ranks of army officers, the bulk of medium grade civil servants, and the professional groups. Under the new social structure the privileged group, both from the financial and social standpoint, consists of military personnel. In all Arab countries the army has come to play a new role and to enjoy new privilege and social stature.

7. *Instruments of Political Action.* An important change has also occurred in the instruments of political action. Lacking an intermediary—political parties and the organs of parliamentary institutions—the common man's medium of political expression became public demonstration. Under control, as in Egypt, this served to strengthen and support the established regime; out of control, as in Iraq, it became an instrument of chaos and devastation. Violence and bloodshed became almost normal features of political life, as did police brutality and military suppression. The

army, formerly a force designed solely for national defense, now became (even to some degree in countries such as Tunisia and Lebanon) the instrument of internal security and political control. It is worth noting that once used on a large scale, as in Iraq under Kassem or in Syria under Hafiz, violence tended to establish itself to the point that in each recurring instance in which it had to be used it appeared in even more forceful and extensive form.

8. *Conspiratorial Action.* Again, with the abolition of open political opposition, conspiracy became a customary method of political action. Conspiratorial action became a familiar part of political behavior with the success of the coup d'état as a means for achieving political change. Apart from the appeal of the effectiveness and speed of this type of action, the grounds of established legitimacy which in the past had discouraged its use were now no longer present. Seen in this light, it is not surprising that the revolutionary regimes established by coup d'état became those most threatened by the counter-coup. Since the first Syrian coup of 1949, political life in the Arab world has been plagued by coup and counter-coup, a pattern which is in great part responsible for the introduction of more stringent measures of control and the spread of coercion and violence in all the countries of the Arab world.

9. *Political Mystification.* Political stability itself was damaged primarily by the rise of army-dominated regimes, which undermined the foundations of legitimacy and radically changed political attitudes and habits. As revolutionary control became firmly established, administrative efficiency increased and with it the power and capacity for control by the new leadership. Once firmly in control of the state, revolutionary leadership became capable of influencing political life in neighboring countries by spreading with money and energy revolutionary ideology and extending its policies by covert means. Under these conditions daily life in the Arab world has become more and more enveloped in mysterious crises, violent upsets, and inexplicable developments, factors which have led to an atmosphere of vagueness, mystery, and insecurity in public life.

10. *Propaganda.* In this atmosphere propaganda has become a major and effective instrument of political action. Exposed to the incessant clamor of radio broadcasts and the daily press, the Arab

citizen is no longer able to think clearly on political matters or to discriminate with assurance between truth and falsehood, reality and fiction. The ever-present threat of violence compounded with omnipresent propaganda has led to the emergence of an almost chronic state of apprehension and excitement. Criteria of objective criticism and serene discussion have been overshadowed by mass hysteria and the monolocutions of propagandists.

REVOLUTIONISM IN TRANSITION

After every coup d'état the successful holders of power have declared a period of transition, to be followed by stability and the resumption of political freedom. Transition is, however, a state of flux which cannot be bridged in accordance with preconceived plans. The upheaval which the process of modernization brings in its train is beyond the will of any leader to bring to an end and beyond the capacity of any ideology to encompass or to harness. Two centuries of domination by Europe have now terminated, but the seeds which Europe had sown have already destroyed the old values and no new foundations have yet been built.

It can perhaps be said that leadership with the vision and will commensurate with the historic moment has not yet emerged. 'Abdul-Nasser, the object of Arab hope in the 1950's, has to many proven to be the Garibaldi of Arab liberation rather than the Bismarck of Arab unity. By the mid-1960's the Arab revolution has not succeeded in formulating a unified ideological basis to which all Arabs can adhere. Indeed, thus far the revolution has succeeded in emphasizing diversity instead of creating unity in the Arab world. Unable to overcome its inner contradictions, the revolution has contributed to the brutalization of politics in the Arab world at the same time that it has given new hope and dignity to the masses of the people. Spontaneous vitalities and organic cohesions, momentarily on the upsurge, have been gradually crushed and have given way to a conformism sustained more by authoritarian control than the unqualified support of those it aimed to serve and uplift.

NOTES

1. *Barnamaj jabhat al-tahrir al-jaza'iriyyah* [Program of the FLN], text in *watha'iq wa dirasat,* Vol. III (Beirut, 1962).
2. *Al-mithaq: qaddamahu al-ra'is Jamal 'Abdul Nasser lilmu'tamar*

al-watani lilqiwa al-sha'biyyah [The Pact: Presented to the National Congress of Popular Forces by President Jamal 'Abdul Nasser] (Cairo, 1962).

3. *Al-muntalaqat al-nathariyyah* [The Ideological Starting Points], partial text in *al-Nahar* (Beirut, October 28, 1963).
4. *Mithaq,* p. 62.
5. *Ibid.,* p. 65.
6. *Barnamaj,* p. 116.
7. *Muntalaqat,* "Resolution No. 2."
8. *Ibid.,* "Resolution No. 15."
9. *Ibid.,* "Resolution No. 14."
10. *Mithaq,* p. 134.
11. *Ibid.,* pp. 136-137.
12. *Ibid.,* p. 137.
13. *Barnamaj,* p. 128.
14. *Muntalaqat,* "Resolution No. 24."

VII. The Language of Politics

THE ARABIC LANGUAGE PLAYS A MAJOR ROLE IN THE POLITICAL life of the Arab world. The language of the Qur'an and the vehicle of classical poetry, it retains quasi-religious undertones and is full of the imagery of medieval Islamic society. Though basically unchanged in structure since Muhammad's time, modern Arabic has been simplified to meet the requirements of the modern world and has developed into a fairly supple vehicle of communication.

In political life Arabic is a most effective instrument of influence and persuasion. When translated into another tongue, however, it loses much of its spell. Although meaning may be faithfully reproduced, hidden implications and psychological associations are often lost.

In public speeches effect is created not so much by reasoning and explication as by repetition and intonation. Indeed, a speaker trying to sway an audience seldom expresses his ideas directly or succinctly; meaning is *conveyed* rather than directly or precisely expressed, and is always couched in terminology that evokes emotional rather than rational responses.

The following excerpt from a speech delivered by Nasser in Damascus on March 11, 1959, will provide some idea of this elusive character of the language as an instrument of political influence. Translated literally, these words appear colorless, almost without meaning or issue. To the Damascene audience, however, to which this speech was addressed, each phrase was highly significant, and cheered with great excitement.

> Fellow Countrymen,
>
> When we took it upon ourselves to raise high the banner of Arab nationalism and defend its call; when we chose the difficult, hard way, the way of defending the whole of the Arab nation, working for it in its entirety, of Arab unity and Arab nationalism, we knew that this way might be a rough one to travel, that it might

> be easier if we chose one of an isolationist policy, a road with a policy that was indeed selfish, a policy that was based largely on ignoring whatever happened in other Arab countries. We knew that such a policy would be easier at the outset, but that eventually it would hand over one Arab country after another to its enemies, that such a divided Arab nation would not achieve solidarity, would inevitably surrender to imperialism; so all of us, each and every one of the sons of this nation, preferred the rough, hard way, the way to Arab unity and solidarity, and resolved to raise the banner of Arab nationalism and exert every effort to thoroughly consolidate it. . . .[1]

Arabic is eminently suited for diplomacy; behind the formulas of politeness and ceremony, intention is easily concealed and meaning only obliquely revealed. By the same token, it is often incapable of precision and clarity and provides for long-windedness and, often, misunderstanding. This is probably one reason why political discussions in the Arab world are usually extremely prolonged and seem never to be quite conclusive.[2]

While Arabic has undergone a process of simplification with the spread of education and growth of mass communication, a "medial" Arabic, neither rigidly classical nor fully colloquial, has developed. As a result, communication in the daily press and radio have been greatly facilitated and the political orator has found a new and easy language. It is significant that use of a combined spoken dialect and "medial" Arabic, rather than the formal, classical language, arose chiefly during the revolution in Egypt, starting with Naguib and Nasser. This departure had tremendous impact on the masses who, addressed for the first time in their own spoken language, felt an unprecedented kinship with the new leadership. In this sense the revolution itself brought this new facility and ease to the Arabic language and enabled the rise of a truly mass press and popular literature. More important perhaps, it removed a profound psychological barrier separating the illiterate masses from the educated classes of society and created on the political plane a new sense of unity and belonging.

The following terms are a fairly representative cross-section of political vocabulary in the Arab world. It is to be noted that these terms are common currency in all classes of Arab society. The attempt here is to provide not only the literal meaning of each term but also to indicate briefly some of the psychological associations it may have and to point out the varieties of nuance or implication that each may possess in the given context.

FATHERLAND, *watan,* gained its modern meaning from and is equivalent to the French *patrie*. The term becomes precise only in its proper context. For the Algerian, for example, it automatically refers to the Algerian fatherland. Used by an Arab nationalist in Syria the term would in most instances refer to the Arab fatherland, including all of the Arab world. In Arab nationalist parlance the adjective Arab or Greater Arab is usually appended to *watan*—*al-watan al-ʿarabi* or *al-watan al-ʿarabi al-kabir*—signifying the totality of the Arabic-speaking world. Thus the Baʿth party defines the Arab fatherland as that area

> which is inhabited by the Arab nation, extending from the Taurus mountains to the Pusht-i-Kuh mountains, to the Gulf of Basra, to the Arabian Sea, the Abyssinian Mountains, the Great Desert, the Atlantic Ocean, and the Mediterranean Sea.[3]

To the Syrian Nationalist party, on the other hand, the fatherland is the Syrian fatherland. "It is that geographic environment in which the Syrian nation evolved;" its boundaries extend

> from the Taurus Range in the northwest and the Zagros Mountains in the northeast to the Suez Canal and the Red Sea in the south and include the Sinai Peninsula and the Gulf of Aqaba, and from the Syrian (Mediterranean) Sea in the west, including the island of Cyprus, to the arch of the Arabian Desert and the Persian Gulf in the east.[4]

In North Africa the Maghrib constitutes a *watan* distinct from that represented by the national boundaries of each state as well as from the Greater Arab fatherland.

PATRIOTISM, *wataniyyah,* derives from watan and should not be confused with *qawmiyyah* (nationalism), derived from *qawm* (people or national community). Patriotism applies within a state's boundaries, whereas nationalism applies to a community that often transcends the confines of a state. The distinction is perhaps made a little clearer when we learn that the adjective *watani* usually denotes "national" rather than "nationalist"; hence, for example, "national economy" (*aliqtisad al-watani*), but "nationalist principles" (*al-mabadiʾ al-qawmiyyah*). *Wataniyyah* usually stands for local nationalism (e.g., Egyptian or Algerian nationalism) as against regional (e.g., Fertile Crescent, Maghribi, or pan-Arab) nationalism.

ARAB NATIONALISM, *al-qawmiyyah al-'arabiyyah,* originated in Syria before World War I and spread throughout the Arab world after World War II. The most sophisticated articulation of the doctrine of Arab nationalism is probably that given by the Socialist Arab Ba'th party. But Arab nationalism does not constitute a single political creed: there is no unanimity as to its basic principles, much less on the manner in which its goals and objectives are to be achieved. Under the leadership of Gamal 'Abdul-Nasser, a mass nationalist movement emerged which attracted the allegiance of Arabs from Morocco to Iraq. Known as "Nasserism" (see below), this movement was not organized into a political party but was sustained by the leadership and articulation which Nasser gave it. In isolating the fundamental elements underpinning the sentiment of Arab nationalism, two elements emerge to constitute a common denominator to all schools and outlooks within Arab nationalism: the concept of Arabism and the idea of unity.

ARABISM, *'urubah,* is a quasi-mystical term denoting the essence of being an Arab—the sense of belonging to the Arab nation, the possession of Arabic as mother tongue, the fact of having been born an Arab in an Arab land, being a Muslim. The Ba'th definition omits the last category: "An Arab is a person whose mother tongue is Arabic, who has lived or who looks forward to living on Arab soil and who believes in being a member of the Arab nation." [5] *'Urubah* implies pride in being the inheritor of Arab culture and recipient of the Muslim heritage; it also involves an awareness of a special destiny; thus,

> the Arab nation has an immortal mission which has manifested itself in renewed and complete forms in the different stages of history and which aims at reviving human values, encouraging human development, and promoting harmony and cooperation among the nations [of the world].[6]

In this sense, *'urubah* is neither racial nor religious in essence, but fundamentally cultural and spiritual. It bestows on the sentiment of nationalism a broad cultural base which, like the humanistic nationalism of mid-nineteenth century Europe, frees it from the narrow limits of state or race and enables it to espouse universalism and humanism as basic components.

UNITY, *wihdah,* is implicit in the feeling and awareness of Arabism: it involves political unity, but also the aspiration for a more profound unity transcending the merely political or economic. This has deep psychological roots that must be sought in the idea of the Muslim community advanced by Muhammad's early teachings and embodied in the community of his first followers. Arabism posits the indivisibility of the Arab nation; the longing for *wihdah* reflects the will to restore to wholeness what has been violated by history, adversity, and accident. Among Arab nationalists there is absolute unanimity as to Arabism and unity, but not as to their doctrinal content or the concrete means whereby they should be implemented. Thus Nasser, Hussein, and the Ba'th party, for instance, can sincerely proclaim their adherence to Arab nationalism and actively strive for realizing its objectives, but still be enemies. The conflict over methods and means does not nullify the existence of profound ideological agreement—which accounts at least in part for the swiftness with which enemies become friends and friends suddenly turn into enemies in the Arab world. In North Africa Arab nationalism is a relatively recent but growing force, especially in Algeria. Among the masses the feeling of Arab brotherhood is still basically Islamic in character. Among the elite the goal of Maghribi unity and the concept of Africanism constitute strong forces that compete with the movement of Arab nationalism and Arab unity.

NASSERISM, *al-Nasiriyyah,* a term originally coined by Nasser's enemies, has come to refer to the movement created by Gamal 'Abdul-Nasser in the Arab world. It consists of various groups and parties that believe Arab nationalism can succeed only under Nasser's leadership and therefore support his policies and uphold his leadership. It is interesting to note that Nasserism exists only outside of Egypt. Its units lack any form of central organization and represent an emotional trend rather than a regimented and coordinated movement.

FEDERAL UNION, *wihdah ittihadiyyah,* is a cumbersome construction in Arabic designed to make clear the distinction between "unity" and "federal unity." It gained currency after the dissolution of the Syrian-Egyptian union in 1961 and was officially used in the unity talks of March-April 1963. It is significant that Nasser did not approve of the term.[7] It has become current, nevertheless.

INDEPENDENCE, *istiqlal,* was the overshadowing goal of every Arab country until it had been achieved. It meant getting rid of foreign domination, reasserting mastery in one's own country, and attaining a position of equality with other independent nations.

SOVEREIGNTY, *siyadah,* represents the full possession of independence. It is not enough to be recognized as "independent," as, for example, Iraq and Egypt were independent in the interwar period. Sovereignty is the unfettered exercise of national will in international affairs, but it also signifies being uncommitted to any great power.

DIGNITY, *karamah,* is implicit in being truly independent and sovereign. For Arabs it represents one of the highest values on the personal as well as the collective levels. For the individual it sums up the totality of his worth as a man. It manifests itself not merely in bearing or in external form of conduct; it consists primarily in a subjective sense of self-esteem—to lose dignity is to lose self-respect. Projected toward the collectivity, national dignity becomes the view that society has of itself. Any violation of it is violation of something fundamental, judged in terms that transcend merely empirical consequences. The greatest violation of national dignity is subjugation to a foreign master, hence the profound mortification of Arabs under European domination and their mystical pride and attachment to their inner identity as Arabs.

HONOR, GLORY, IMMORTALITY, *sharaf, majd, khulud* are three principal values that occupy a dominant place in Arab imagination and play an important role in influencing attitude and behavior. In public life, every political act is viewed somehow in these ultimate terms. Hence, preserving national honor or achieving glory and immortality are involved in the least act touching upon national life. Political life is thus peopled by heroes or cowards, good men or bad men, giants or dwarfs. More important, perhaps, is the fact that nothing and no one possesses permanence. Absolute values become relative to the given situation, subject to the prevailing mood or emotion. Thus Kassem can be the "immortal leader" one day, and the next the villainous traitor. In a sense, while the values that describe and motivate action often have more force in influencing behavior than do practical considerations, they are just as often empty shells, containing no precise and defineable meaning; they tend to exert pressure on the collective imagination by force of habit and the fascination of the Arabic language.

TRAITOR, AGENT, LACKEY, *kha'in, 'amil, ma'jur,* are principal detractors that dominate political vocabulary and have perhaps the highest frequency rate in political speeches, radio broadcasts, and newspaper columns. A traitor is usually a political enemy; the highest form of treason is to be an "agent" or "lackey" of imperialism. Thus, from a speech by Nasser:

> [Our] enemies are represented by imperialism, by its lackeys and agents; [by] those who want to subjugate us to the foreigner; [by] traitorous people from among our citizens who work for the foreigner in order to subjugate our country at a cheap price, for purely personal reasons. . . .[8]

IMPERIALISM, *isti'mar,* is a key term, symbolizing all that is hateful and repugnant to Arab nationalism. Neoimperialism—indirect political or economic influence by a big foreign power—has become the object of attack as being an even more pernicious form of interference and exploitation. Traitors are easily bought by the imperialists, and agents and lackeys are easy to recruit. The exact objectives and goals of imperialism—whether British, French, Russian, or American—are vague; the prevailing impression, however, is that it aims at dominating the Arab world in order to reestablish political control, to exploit the oil, to gain strategic positions. In its effort to achieve these goals imperialism must fight Arab nationalism and try to block the movement of Arab unity.

COMMUNISM, *shuyu'iyyah,* is a "bad" name in Arabic; it generates mistrust rather than fear. For the masses, Communism constitutes an alien movement with an unintelligible philosophy; for the nationalists, it is an antinationalist doctrine and is therefore opposed. Though the revolutionary socialists implicitly accept certain aspects of theoretical Marxism, they are adamantly opposed to Communist totalitarian dogmatism, the theory of class struggle, and the views on private property. As an internal political movement, Communism has earned the antagonism of all parties and groups in the Arab world, from the extreme socialist left to the traditionalist right. The various small Communist parties of the Arab world have always been regarded as instruments of a foreign power, which has added to public mistrust and has led to their suppression in every country in the Arab world.

"ANTI-ARABISM," *shu'ubiyya,* is an important term derived from early Arab history dating back to the period in which non-Arab Muslims (mainly Persians) attacked Arabism and claimed superiority over and separateness from the Arabs. In the modern context, it is an effective term usually used against political movements, groups, or individuals who do not adhere to the principle of Arab nationalism or who affirm local (territorial) or regional nationalism, or who are not actively in favor of total Arab unity. All such parties, groups, and individuals are viewed as enemies of Arab nationalism, traitors of the revolution, and natural allies of neoimperialism. The term carries with it a profound and deeply wounding insult to anyone who considers himself an Arab, for it separates the "authentic" Arab from the "quasi-Arab" (normally differentiated in terms of religion or ethnic origin). Its particular effectiveness is due to the fact that it can be used indirectly to create suspicion and provide insinuations which need not be clearly stated. The Voice of the Arabs, for example, in attacking Michel 'Aflaq, the founder and intellectual spokesman of the Ba'th, would call him a *shu'ubi,* thus indirectly reminding the listener of the fact that he is a Christian, consequently not altogether an Arab, and thus impugning his good faith and nationalist integrity.

OPPORTUNISM, *al-intihaziyyah,* implicitly refers to the prerevolutionary type of political corruption; hence, an opportunist in the context of the revolution is either willingly or in effect a traitor, a stooge, or an agent of imperialism.

REACTIONISM, *al-raj'iyyah,* includes all the antirevolutionary classes and groups—the big merchants, the landed aristocracy, the upper urban classes, the conservative right. The term gained meaning and significance as socialist ideology spread. It is used only in a derogatory sense, and has come to carry considerable weight.

FEUDALISM, *al-iqta'iyyah,* signifies reaction, although it is most often used in the literal sense, denoting economic as well as political oppression. Monarchical regimes are branded as both reactionary and feudalistic.

PROGRESSIVENESS, *al-taqaddumiyyah,* is reserved to revolutionary nationalism, and to movements of the left that stand opposed to traditionalism and the *status quo*. It is important to note that progress in Arabic still has some of the magic associated with the optimistic nineteenth century sense of the term.

CONSPIRACY, PLOT, *mu'amara.* Arab political climate is heavy with conspiracies and plots, for political opposition is mostly underground and secretiveness is the normal condition of political life. Thus the whispering campaign is as effective as radio broadcasts, and news is not so much reporting as reading meaning into developments and events. Just as the obvious is never taken at face value, so the hidden motive is always the object of examination and questioning. The line separating credulity from cynicism is often too thin even from the standpoint of those who are engaged in political action. The mystery permeating this atmosphere induces suspicion and mistrust; the ordinary man sees a plot behind every shift in every policy, every decision or development, whether within the army, by a foreign power, or by a political group. There is an oil conspiracy, a Communist conspiracy, and an imperialist conspiracy.

REVOLUTION, *al-thawrah,* is a "good" word in Arabic; it has a sense of inner liberation and restoration of self-respect associated with it regardless of the actual reality of any particular revolution in the Arab world. Its more precise implications are rapid political change, economic reform, social equality, power—but, significantly, hardly its literal meaning, namely, popular uprising against a tyrannical government. The Algerians preferred to refer to the Algerian revolution as the Algerian war, reserving the term revolution for the socialist regime established after the revolution. By the same token, every government established by coup d'état proclaimed itself harbinger of the revolution, the beginning of a new revolutionary era. Until the Second World War *al-thawrah* referred to a number of revolutions—the Arab revolt of 1916, the Egyptian revolution of 1919, the Syrian revolution of 1925. With the coming of the postwar era in North Africa and the coups d'état in the Arab East, "revolution" began to acquire a new and broader connotation.

Thus although each revolutionary regime would have its own *thawrah* (even every counter-coup in Syria and Iraq proclaimed its own genuine *thawrah*), the term became generally understood as the revolutionary wave, involving social and economic revolution as well as political. In this sense, the revolution without qualification represents the search for social justice of the core revolutionary states of the Arab world.

PEOPLE, *al-sha'b, al-jamahir al-sha'biyyah,* in revolutionary parlance has acquired a distinct significance through its association with the revolution. The people, or literally the masses of the people, are no longer the object of contempt. The abstract concept which the term conveys is employed to lay claim to legitimacy. It is significant to note that the "will of the people" signifies the "will of the *common* people," excluding the higher and better-off classes. Hence, revolutionary leadership upholds the "people," chiefly the workers and peasants, as the base and mainspring of revolution.

LEADER, *za'im,* has two distinct significations, local "boss" and national leader. Thus in elections in Lebanon practically all candidates are called *za'im* by their followers; Kassem approved the unofficial title, "sole leader," *al-za'im al-awahad.* A further distinction is between *za'im,* in the sense of national leader, and *ra'is,* head, president, or chairman, terms of more formal and specific connotations. Thus Nasser is *za'im* of the Arabs, and *ra'is* of the UAR; and Bourghiba *za'im* of the Tunisian people, and the official *ra'is* of the Neo-Destour party. The one instance in which *za'im* was used in a strict functional sense denoting both leader and chief was in the Syrian Nationalist party, whose leader and founder was called simply *al-za'im.*

STATE, *al-dawlah,* may also mean government, regime, power, administration. The state, in the national sense, did not come into being in the Arab world until very recent times. The state is seen in terms of its political leadership and its power of coercion rather than as an independent structure represented by institutions and laws that have permanence and validity outside individuals and considerations of power used by government. The state has as its most permanent circumstance the bureaucracy, the only institution that has resisted change and survived upheaval and coup d'état. Still, especially in revolutionary regimes, there is no clear distinction in popular consciousness between the state and the individual or individuals who wield the powers of the state.

NOTES

1. The writer heard the speech broadcast from Damascus; the full text in Muhammad Khalil, *The Arab States and the Arab League* (Beirut, 1962), Vol. II, p. 946.

2. See, for example, *Minutes of Unity Discussions* [in Arabic] (Cairo, 1963), p. 13.

3. *Constitution of the Socialist Arab Resurrection Party,* text in Khalil, *op. cit.,* I, pp. 663-670; see "General Principles," Article 7.

4. *The Principles of the Social Syrian Nationalist Party* (Beirut, n.d.), "Fifth Principle."

5. *Constitution of the Socialist Arab Resurrection Party, op. cit.,* "General Principles," Article 10.

6. *Ibid.,* "Third Principle."

7. *Minutes of Unity Discussions, op. cit.,* p. 82.

8. Speech by Nasser in Damascus, March 15, 1959; text in Khalil, *op. cit.,* II, p. 956.

Part Two

I. Statements and Speeches

No. 1 Arab University Graduates Conference: Resolutions on Outstanding Problems

Main resolutions taken at the first inter-Arab conference of college and university graduates held in Beirut, June 23-June 25, 1954. Mu'tamar al-khirrijin al-da'im liqadaya al-watan al-'arabi [*Permanent Conference of University Graduates for the Problems of the Arab Fatherland*] (*first session; Beirut, 1954*).*

POLITICAL RESOLUTIONS

[Steps toward the] realization of Arab Unity. . . .

1. Eliminate the use of passports for Arab subjects travelling in the Arab world to enable them, including the Palestine refugees, to move freely in all Arab countries using identity cards only.
2. Extend to subjects of all the Arab states the right to own property in any Arab country.
3. Extend to all subjects of the Arab states the right to work in any Arab country on a level of equality with the citizens of that country.
4. Jewish subjects are to be excepted from the above.

THE PALESTINE PROBLEM

1. Concentrate the Palestine refugees in the nonoccupied part of Palestine and along the borders of the Arab countries adjoining Palestine and assure them work and the means for their defense. . . .
2. Recruit and train the refugees to strengthen the [Jordanian] National Guard as a temporary defense force, and to guard the borders [with Israel] in conjunction with the armies of the adjoining Arab countries as well as with those of nonadjoining countries.

* Selections in this and the following chapters are translated by the author, unless otherwise indicated.

3. Tighten the economic blockade of Israel and deal mercilessly with traitors, smugglers, and spies.

4. Establish an information agency to enlighten world public opinion on the justice of the Arab demands and to reveal Zionist atrocities. (pp. 79-80)

SOCIAL RESOLUTIONS

1. Recommend to the Arab states as the basis of government and governmental institutions the establishment of the right of popular self-rule.

2. Recommend to the Arab states the signing of the [U.N.] Charter of Human Rights so that this international instrument may become equivalent to national law, binding citizens and governments alike.

3. Recommend to the Arab states the drawing up of laws covering political, economic, and social matters, that would safeguard the intrinsic human rights of citizens, particularly the right to life and all that derives from it, and economic and social rights.

4. Recommend to the Arab states the drawing up of charters safeguarding public freedoms, particularly the freedom of thought, conviction, and religious belief and the freedom of opinion, expression, and association; and to substitute these charters for all [existing] laws that violate human rights or the rights of citizens. (p. 86)

No. 2 Hasan al-Banna: On the Doctrine of the Muslim Brothers

The following selections are taken from speeches and writings by the founder and "Supreme Guide" of the Muslim Brotherhood, delivered or written shortly after the end of the Second World War. Risalat al-mu'tamar al-khamis [*Message of the Fifth Conference*] (*Cairo, n.d.*).

MEANING OF ISLAM

1. We believe that the doctrines and teachings of Islam are all-comprehensive and govern the affairs of men in this world and the

next. Those who believe that these doctrines and teachings apply only to spiritual matters and to religious worship are mistaken, for Islam is at once . . . religion and state, spirit and work, holy book and sword. . . .

2. The [Muslim] Brothers believe, moreover, that the basis and source of Islam are the book of Allah [Qu'ran] (may it be blessed and elevated) and the Sunna of the Prophet (may Allah's blessings and peace be on him); if the nation holds on to them it will never lose its way. . . .

3. The Muslim Brothers also believe that Islam as a universal religion regulates all the affairs of man's life, that it applies to all nations and all peoples, and that it is for all ages and for all time. . . .

This is why Islam has never failed to benefit from any order or system which does not contradict its fundamental principles or its basic laws. (pp. 10-14)

FORCE AND REVOLUTION

Many people ask: is it the intention of the Muslim Brothers to use force in achieving their purpose and reaching their goals? Do the Muslim Brothers think of a general revolution against the political or social order in Egypt?

. . . I say to these questioners that the Muslim Brothers will use physical force only when nothing else will do, and then only when they are convinced they have perfected their faith and unity. [But] when they [decide to] use force they will be honorable and frank and will give advance warning. . . . As for revolution, the Muslim Brothers do not think of it or depend on it or believe in its benefits and results. Nevertheless they have been frank in telling every government that has taken over power in Egypt that if conditions remained as they were and if those responsible failed to find speedy solutions to these problems, this would inevitably lead to a revolution which would not be the making of the Muslim Brothers or the response to their call. . . . (pp. 34, 36-37)

THE MUSLIM BROTHERS AND GOVERNMENT

Another group of people ask: Is it part of the program of the Muslim Brothers to take over the government . . . ? The Muslim

Brothers do not demand power for themselves; if they find anyone capable of carrying this burden and of fulfilling the trust of government in accordance with a program based on Islam and the Qur'an, then they *will* be his soldiers, supporters, and helpers. But if they do not find such a man, then power is included in their program, and they would strive to seize it from the hands of any government that does not fulfill Allah's commands. . . . (pp. 37-38)

NATIONAL, ARAB, AND ISLAMIC UNITY

. . . The Muslim Brothers love their country and are anxious to preserve its unity; they find nothing wrong for any man in being loyal to his country, dying for the sake of his people, and wishing for his fatherland every glory and every honor, and every pride. All this is from the particular standpoint of nationalism [*min wijhat al-qawmiyyah al-khassah*]. . . .

The Arabs are the core and guardians of Islam. . . . Arab unity is an essential prerequisite for the restoration of Islam's glory, the reestablishment of the Muslim state, and the consolidation of Muslim power. This is why it is the duty of every Muslim to work for the revival and support of Arab unity—this is the position of the Muslim Brothers with regard to Arab unity.

It remains to define our position regarding Islamic unity. The truth is that just as Islam is a religious faith and a system of worship, it is also patriotism and nationality. . . . As such, Islam does not recognize geographic frontiers nor the distinctions of nationality or race, but considers all Muslims as one single nation and the Islamic homeland as one single territory, no matter how far flung or remote the countries of which it is composed may be. . . . It should thus be evident that the Muslim Brothers owe respect to their own particular nationalism, Egyptian nationalism, which constitutes the primary basis of the revival that they seek. After that they support Arab unity, which constitutes the second link in the movement of revival; and finally they strive for the Islamic League, [al-jami'ah al-islamiyyah], which constitutes the perfect enclosure for the larger Islamic homeland. It is only left to say that the Brothers desire the good of the whole world and indeed call for world unity, which is the purpose and final goal of Islam. . . . (pp. 45, 47-48, 49-50)

No. 3 Michel 'Aflaq: On Militant Arab Nationalism

Selections from a collection of articles and speeches by the founder of the Ba'th party. Fi sabil al-Ba'th [*For the Resurrection*] (*Beirut, 1959*).

OUR SOCIALISM IS NATIONALIST

When we say that we are in need of an Arab Socialism, all we mean is that attention should be given to the special circumstances that pertain to us as Arabs in this phase of our history. We all agree as to the principle of socialism, but not as to the manner in which it should be applied or to the place it should occupy in our [national] life. We cannot accept the view of Western socialism that nationalism is merely a transient phase in the process of economic evolution. On the contrary, socialism must be suited to our nation and to our political struggle, and not become an instrument of conspiracy against our fatherland, or a means of internal division and strife, or a screen for antinationalist maneuvers.

We want socialism to serve our nationalist cause, to increase our intellectual daring, and to strengthen our call for individual freedom and the fruitfulness and richness of our spirit—not to kill our new freedom in its cradle. . . . (1946; p. 89)

COMMUNISM IS A DANGER

. . . What would become of Arab thought if it were overcome by an artificial philosophy such as Communist socialism . . . with all that is false and distorted in this philosophy? If we adopt [Communist] socialism as our philosophy of life . . . then we shall destroy the future of Arab thought and its freedom with our own hands. (1946; pp. 88-89)

UNITY

. . . In short, brothers, the battle for unity cannot—according to our doctrine and our view and our struggle—be separated from the battle for freedom and liberation and socialism, nor should it be separated under any circumstances. I believe we define the true [meaning] of this battle when we say that it will determine the degree of revolutionary spirit in individuals and groups, as well as in the nation at large, during this phase. . . . (1958; p. 243)

THE ARABS AND THE WEST

. . . Europe is as fearful of Islam today as she has been in the past. She now knows that the strength of Islam (which in the past expressed that of the Arabs) has been reborn and has appeared in a new form: in Arab nationalism. For this reason she employs all her weapons against this new force. We see Europe befriending traditional Islam and giving it support. That kind of Islam—superficial worship, vague and colorless values—is being gradually Europeanized (*tafarnuj*). . . .

The day will come when the nationalists will find themselves the only defenders of true Islam, and they will have to create in it new meaning if they are determined to preserve good reason for the survival of the Arab nation. (1943; p. 47)

No. 4 Antun Sa'adah: On the Syrian Nationalist Movement

Antun Sa'adah founded the Syrian National party in Lebanon in 1932. By "Syria" is here meant the Fertile Crescent area, including Lebanon, Syria, Palestine, Transjordan, Iraq, and Kuwait. The following excerpts are from editorials written in 1949, the year that Sa'adah was summarily executed in Lebanon. Al-nizam al-Jadid [New Order, *monthly journal*] *November 1950; February 1951.*

REALISTIC ARABISM

The realistic Arabism which the Syrian Nationalist movement advocates is the [sound] nationalist principle for the Arab world; it is altogether different from that which bases itself on abstractions such as "Arab nation," "Arab nationalism," "Arab fatherland," "Arab unity." We are realists. We look upon the Arab world realistically, not in terms of dreams and illusions. The reality of the Arab world is that it is composed of diverse communities, peoples, and nations. We do not try to delude the people by saying that it is possible to transform these into one people and one nation through the bonds of language and religion, or on the basis of the community of Arab blood. . . .

This illusory brand of Arabism, which by claiming that it is possible to effect such transformation leads the Syrian nation to believe in illusion . . . is precisely the kind of Arab nationalist [doctrine] against which the Syrian National movement fights. It is the doctrine which (as it sought to realize Arab unity) has caused the loss of Cilicia, Alexandretta, and Palestine! (pp. 43-44)

THE COMMUNIST THREAT

Workers and Farmers of Syria:

The call which Communism directs to you, to abandon nationalism and love of fatherland, is really asking you to give up your right to sovereignty over the very resources which are the conditions of your livelihood and well-being. . . .

Equitable distribution of scarcity and poverty will not save us from prostration and misery, no matter how just the distribution. Nationalism and mastery over the national resources are the foundations of our socialism. . . .

Our national struggle, O workers and farmers, is against two enemies: against domestic feudalism and capitalism backed by foreign feudal and capitalistic forces, and against the political feudalism of Communism and the economic imperialism of capitalism. . . . (pp. 73-74)

We Cannot Escape Victory!

Throughout the fatherland members of the party are asked: Where are you? The people are waiting for you! You are the nation's only hope!

Yes, the whole Syrian nation awaits the hour of victory of the Syrian Nationalist movement. . . .

Nothing in the world daunts this movement, for it is a strong and triumphant movement. . . . (pp. 22-23)

No. 5 Habib Bourghiba: On "Constitutional Socialism"

Excerpts from a speech delivered at a youth rally in Tunis on July 29, 1963. Al-Fikr, *Vol. IX, No. 3 (December, 1963), pp. 2-3.*

. . . Our method—I mean constitutional socialism—is derived from our Tunisian situation; to meet this situation we have set up a basic goal: the creation of a better society by raising the standard of living, improving production, and establishing equitable distribution [of wealth]. After assuring ourselves of our aim we have proceeded to find the ways that lead to it; our search has directed us to this fundamental general principle: that the Tunisian citizen in this new era is a partner of every other member of society; it is thus that our socialism is derived, not as a reaction to capitalism, but to extreme individualism. It became amply clear that a way of life based on narrow individualism, allowing everyone to do what he pleased, was not good or profitable; it became necessary to change it and to find the means whereby individuals could be guided and their efforts combined into an effective collective effort. We are all responsible for this land and we should live in it with dignity. We have called this approach "socialism"; the individual is no longer equated with the nation as a whole nor considered a final goal; we have become a complete social organism. The role of the state in society is to prevent the individual members of society from going astray and thus causing harm to the public good. The duty of the state is to look after its citizens, employing for this purpose all the resources and foresight at its disposal, combating injustice, exploitation, monopoly, and everything which is contrary to the values of justice, freedom, and brotherhoood. . . . And contrary to the views of Karl Marx, who believes class war to be inevitable, our effort is set on fighing evil, not persons. . . .

No. 6 Ahmed Ben Bella: On the Revolution, Arabism, and Socialism

Selections from speeches delivered in 1962 and 1963; 'Abdul Rahman Mahmoud al-Hiss, al-jaza'ir fi ma'rakat al-bina' [*Algeria in the Battle of Reconstruction*] (*Beirut, 1963*).

THE PEOPLE'S DEMOCRATIC REPUBLIC OF ALGERIA

In using this name we did not intend to belong to any particular camp, neither Eastern nor Western. We intend only to remove the vast discrepancies between the different classes of society and to prevent the exploitation of one group by another.

[Algeria] is a "democratic republic" because we believe in the democratic system that provides for freedom of speech and discussion and investigation, and [contributes] to the improvement of the common lot and the strengthening of internal security and world peace.

It is a "people's republic" because it is the embodiment of the will of the people, who have paid dearly for its freedom and independence, sacrificing many hundreds of thousands of victims, but who have succeeded—thanks be to God—in achieving their national goals.

And it is an "Arab republic" because it is a possessor of the Arab [cultural] legacy and has been molded by it. Algeria, like its sister Arab republics, is responsible for deepening Arab national consciousness and obligated to serve the interests of Arabism everywhere. (p. 88)

ARAB UNITY

No one can foresee how relations [among the Arab countries] will evolve in the near future. All there is to say is that we believe in the necessity of getting closer in brotherhood, and in strengthening these relations to the maximum. As for the moment for union or federation, time will decide that—time is the physician that dispenses the proper medicine at the proper time.

Unity itself depends on a condition essential to its realization: it is for Arabs to prepare the ground in each Arab country, to mold each society within a unified framework of unified tendencies, then to prepare it to embark on this unity in a strong, assured way.

The desire to unite the countries of Arab North Africa is a natural and logical inclination; indeed it is a blessed call, provided that it shall not obstruct the larger unity between all the Arab countries. (pp. 88-89)

ANNIVERSARY OF THE ALGERIAN REVOLUTION

. . . Our goal is to put an end to all distinctions and to establish a revolutionary Arab socialism. The starting point of our social revolution is agricultural reform, which must constitute a genuine revolution. Through this reform, which will be put into effect soon, land will be distributed among one million farmers. . . .

A million martyrs have given their lives not only for the sake of the flag; they have sacrificed their lives for the socialist revolution, which is Arab in character and which shall preserve our national identity. The sacrifices made by our people were not only for the sake of freedom and social justice, but also and above all in defense of our national existence as Arabs, which colonialism has sought to tear apart and destroy. This doctrinal basis of our struggle and sacrifice was the basis not only of the seven years of revolution, but that of all the wars of liberation which our people have waged from Amir 'Abdul Qadir, al-Maqrani, Bu Ma'izzah, and the sons of Sidi al-Shaikh, to this day. . . .

No. 7 Hassan II: On the New Constitution

From a speech delivered on the eve of the constitutional referendum (December 6, 1962), text translated and published by the Embassy of the Kingdom of Morocco, Washington, D.C., 1963.

Faithful People,

Seven years ago the late King, Mohammed V, my august father, may his soul rest with God, was returned to the love of his faithful people. A resuscitated people regained its faith, its dignity, and its independence. To the black night filled with shadows and nightmares came the bright new day. A new Morocco was about to be born, constructed by all and for all. And from that instant, His Majesty, Mohammed V, finally able to realize one of his most cherished wishes, decided to give Morocco democratic institutions, institutions which, moreover, were only the first but necessary consequence of recovered Independence and National Sovereignty. . . .

People of Morocco,

Dominated by the great shadow of the one we loved so much, filled with his thoughts and memory, I have personally conceived of and established the project of a Constitution for the Kingdom which I am now going to submit to you for approval. . . .

The Constitution is first of all a solemn proclamation of the political Rights and Liberties of the Moroccan citizen. . . .

The Constitution also creates assemblies, elected by the people in order to be the spokesmen for their aspirations and needs, and in order to insure that the government accomplish its task well. . . .

[It] is finally a government responsible to the Assemblies which will in turn be able to cause it to resign if it does not follow an established policy. . . .

But in order that the Institutions thus designed may function in the best conditions for the good of the people and the grandeur of the Fatherland, in order that the authority and continuance of the State be maintained through adversity, it is necessary that your King, guarantor of the Constitution and defender of the rights of everyone, be able, at all times, to control and follow State affairs and, if it should become necessary, with the consent and help of the people, triumph, as in the past, over obstacles which could arise before us.

Thus the Constitution that I have made with my own hands, this Constitution which tomorrow will be distributed throughout the territory of the Kingdom and which, within twenty days, will be submitted to your approval, is above all a renewal of the sacred pact which has always united the People and the King, and which is the very foundation of our success. . . .

No. 8 Gamal 'Abdul-Nasser: On the Achievements of the Egyptian Revolution

Excerpts from a speech delivered at the first meeting of the Egyptian National Assembly in Cairo on March 26, 1964. Partial text, Lisan al-hal (*Beirut, March 28, 1964*).

Fellow citizens, members of the National Assembly:

History and the Revolution have entered this hall before us; both wish to look upon this glorious new scene upon which all eyes are riveted today.

This popular assembly, freely elected by the mass of the people, constitutes a major turning point in the political, social, and national history of this part of the world—where we live and build in the light of the true and the good—a single Arab nation astride the Ocean and the Gulf. This elected assembly is a great and decisive event in the life of the Arab nation.

This road was opened by the will of the people's revolution when it succeeded in crushing imperialism and reaction and capitalist exploitation, and in overthrowing the unholy combines that allied themselves against the people. . . .

The vanguard which emerged in response to the people's call set forth six objectives for its movement:

1. To destroy imperialism and its traitorous Egyptian agents;
2. to eliminate feudalism;
3. to get rid of monopolies and the domination of capitalism;
4. to establish social justice;
5. to build a strong national army; and
6. to introduce a genuine democracy. . . .

The first enemy is imperialism, the second Israel . . . and the third the forces of reaction in the Arab world. . . . The separatist movement which arose in Damascus was able on September 28, 1961, to break up the union of Syria and Egypt; but the revolution in Yemen reversed this course and forced reaction to take the defensive. We have emerged victorious from our courageous confrontation with our enemies and we have achieved something important in reaching our goals—we possess complete clarity. Israel is no longer anything in confronting us, and imperialism has become something else. . . . The old kingdom of princes and pashas and "foreign gentlemen" has disappeared and been replaced by the republic of the peasants and the workers. . . .

After economic development there is the goal of democracy to achieve—to broaden its framework, to deepen its meaning and to complete the construction of the political system of the Socialist Union. . . .

I raise my voice before you now to forewarn you never to put your reliance in one man. The people must remain master and leader, for the people will continue and last more than any leader. I say this realizing full well that you have given me of your support and backing and good will more than I could have ever imagined or dreamed possible. I have given the people my life, but the people have given me what is greater than anyone's life. . . .

No. 9 Fu'ad Shehab: On Lebanese Unity

Excerpts from the first address by General Fu'ad Shehab, Commander in Chief of the Army, upon his election to the presidency of the republic on September 23, 1958, following the end of the Lebanese civil war (May-September 1958); American troops, which had landed in Lebanon in July in response to the former president's request, had not yet been evacuated. English text in Muhammad Khalil, The Arab States and the Arab League (*Beirut, 1962*), *pp. 134-137.*

Honorable Deputies,

There lies between my office as a soldier in the headquarters [of the Lebanese Army], where silence is the companion of duty, and the rostrum of this assembly, where speech is master, a [great] distance which may be the hardest I have been destined to traverse ever since I chose a military career. . . .

While in this position, which fills one's heart with awe of responsibility before God and the fatherland, our thoughts turn, first and foremost, to those Lebanese [citizens] who fell as victims in the [recent] sanguinary days in the life of Lebanon. Let us, thus, stand in humility before their souls and declare that the victims whom Lebanon has offered in her recent crisis, the difficulties and the troubles she has suffered, and the losses she has sustained, shall not be in vain. . . .

The [ability] to set things right and to exercise authority [in] the State throughout the whole of Lebanon requires the disarming of all Lebanese, indiscriminately and uncompromisingly. The restoration of life and activity to Lebanese economy, the reconstruction of what has been damaged in the public resources and landmarks of the country, the elimination of the tension in the relations between Lebanon and some of her sister Arab countries, particularly those adjoining her, and, above all, the achievement of the withdrawal of foreign forces from the territory of the fatherland as soon as possible, are but persistent questions the solution of which demands the full determination of those responsible, together with their greatest firmness and constant vigilance.

There is, however, another aspect of the crisis. This is the breaking up and the estrangement which have occurred among members of the Lebanese family and which are the legacy of the events and days of [that crisis]. I am sure that all Lebanese are feeling sorry for this regrettable state of affairs and aspire to eliminate from their own minds and hearts the [prejudices] which have accumulated there. . . .

At the same time as I take the oath of maintaining the Lebanese Constitution, I pledge myself, and ask you [on your part] to pledge yourselves to be faithful to the unwritten constitution—our National Pact. For it was this [pact] which brought us, and still brings us, together [united as we are] in the belief in Lebanon as [our] beloved, independent, sovereign, and free fatherland. . . .

II. Revolutionary Ideology: FLN, UAR, Ba'th

No. 10 Algeria: FLN Program

On May 27, 1964, the National Council of the Algerian Revolution unanimously adopted a political-economic program, prepared by a special committee, which defined the basic doctrines and goals of the FLN, set forth the principles of the revolution that became the official platform of the Algerian government, and provided the groundwork for the Algerian constitution. Text in watha'iq wa dirasat [*Documents and Studies*], *Vol. III (November 1962), pp. 101-128.*

WAR OF LIBERATION AND THE RESTORATION OF NATIONAL SOVEREIGNTY

On March 19, 1962, a cease-fire was proclaimed, putting an end to a long war of extermination waged by French colonialism against the Algerian people. The cease-fire resulted from an agreement concluded between the Provisional Algerian government and France at Evian, declaring the independence of Algeria and safeguarding its territorial integrity. . . .

The Evian agreement constitutes a political victory for the Algerian people which cannot be reversed, for it has put an end to colonialism and foreign domination. This victory, however, will not make us forget that it [the agreement] is, above all, the product of revolutionary developments and the historic political and social accomplishments of the armed struggle of the Algerian people. The accomplishments of the war of liberation represent the only permanent victory, for they embody the palpable fruits of the struggle and constitute the true guarantee of the fatherland and the revolution.

THE ARMED STRUGGLE AND NATIONAL LIBERALISM

When, on November 1, 1954, the Front of National Liberation embarked on revolutionary action, it viewed armed resistance only from the standpoint of national liberation and did not foresee the different requirements and developments the war would make in the popular consciousness and in Algerian society at large.

1. The FLN was ignorant of the profound revolutionary capabilities of the rural population. The little knowledge it had was of a situation long in a state of stagnation, a situation which the national parties, in their muddled estimation, had always assumed to be so. It is true that the FLN, *avant-garde* in tendency, tried at the beginning to dissociate itself from the ideas and methods of the old parties; but this dissociation could not be genuine and final unless accompanied by ideological distinctions and long-range plans. . . .

The FLN did not concern itself positively with setting up a goal beyond that of the traditional national movement, namely, political independence. It failed, moreover, to foresee the potential significance of two basic problems not even considered by the traditional national movement: first, the character of an anticolonial war in a country with a large proportion of foreigners playing the simultaneous roles of representatives, agents, and assistants of the French colonialism; and secondly, that organization of armed rebellion and recruitment of colonized people—aiming at undermining the long established colonial order—could not be based on vague plans and naive strivings. . . .

Though it may appear contradictory, the masses had a keener sense and comprehension of the uniqueness and spontaneity of the revolutionary dimension of the national struggle than did those who directed and administered [the revolutionary struggle]. These latter usually tended either to underestimate or to exaggerate developments; they cited cases pertaining to other revolutions and conformed blindly to established dogmas. . . .

IDEOLOGICAL BLINDNESS

2. We have seen and still see a dangerous gap between collective consciousness, which has matured through long contact with reality, and [the leadership of] the Liberation Front. Absolutist authority replaced in most cases political responsibility. . . . It

always tried to justify itself; its approach was haughty and condescending.

This attitude of authority toward political responsibility derived from the exigent conditions of the struggle and persisted due to the FLN's lack of firm ideological foundations; this narrowed the concept of authority and power to external manifestations and very quickly led to the dissemination of views and ideas that can be described as contrary to the revolutionary spirit.

FEUDALISM

3. The FLN, despite its violent attack on feudalism and its attempts to uproot the social foundations of the feudal order, did not make any effort to prevent certain aspects of its organization from being contaminated by the feudal spirit. It did not realize that what contributes to survival of feudalism are overconcentration of power, absence of valid criteria [of judgment], and lack of proper political education. Feudalism is not merely what concerns a certain social class . . . ; in the Afro-Asian countries, where it is a relic of the dead and ancient past, feudalism assumes many forms; it [infiltrates] peoples' revolutions that lack ideological consciousness. Just as there is agricultural feudalism, so there is political feudalism—anarchistic cliques of leaders and bosses with followings, clients, and agents. The chief cause of this is the lack of proper democratic education both among the political leaders and the people at large. . . .

BOURGEOIS MENTALITY

4. There is another kind of mentality which we must expose because in the past it has inflicted immeasurable damage on our political life, and today, together with the remnants of feudalism, it is about to inflict the same damage on the revolution—namely, the mentality of the small bourgeoisie. The absence of rigorous norms in the FLN has allowed this mentality to infiltrate institutional structures and to affect a large body of our youth. . . .

This mentality, equipped as it is with a borrowed and false intellectualism, has appropriated all sorts of distorted and harmful Western concepts and has created through a new bureaucratic class a vast gulf between [itself] and the masses. . . .

VAGUENESS OF RESPONSIBILITY

5. One of the chief obstacles to the development of an FLN ideology which contributed to many of its shortcomings and adversely influenced the situation in Algeria during the war, was the gap separating the leadership [of the FLN] and the masses. The establishment of FLN headquarters outside Algeria after the third year of conflict (though circumstances required it) cut off the leadership from the situation inside Algeria. This alienation might have undermined the entire movement of liberation. . . .

THE SOCIAL FOUNDATIONS OF THE FLN

What are the social foundations of the FLN?

Above all, the common people—particularly the most persecuted classes:

First, the poverty-stricken peasants . . . the agricultural laborers (permanent and seasonal), the sharecroppers, the small land agents, and the poorer landholders.

Two, the working class, which is relatively small, the "half workers," (*ansaf al-'ummal*) who are more numerous, and the "near-workers" (*shibh al-'ummal*), who are becoming more numerous in the cities and consist mostly of peasants whose lands were confiscated. . . .

Three, a middle social group which includes small manufacturers, professionals, civil servants, small merchants, and a segment of those engaged in free enterprise—a social group which can be called the small bourgeoisie. . . .

Four, a small middle class (bourgeoisie) composed of those owning large commercial and financial interests, big merchants, a very small number of industrialists, and the large landowners and high officials of the colonial administration. . . .

What are the distinctive features of the Algerian Revolution?

The word revolution has often been used out of context and without a precise connotation; the very word revolution was sufficient to bolster the will of the masses, who instinctively gave it a content surpassing that of mere political struggle. What the revolution lacked, and still lacks, is the requisite doctrinal content. . . . [Now] the ideological struggle must take the place of the war for [political] liberation, and [become] . . . a struggle for the realization of the democratic people's revolution. The democratic people's revolution is the militant movement of the aroused Algerian people striving to build a new society and a new state.

A. The Democratic Content

The revolution aims at reestablishing national foundations once independence has been secured; it seeks to do this by reinstating the principles and values that were distorted and mutilated by colonialism. . . . The sense of responsibility, which is the most genuine expression of democracy, must replace feudal authority and imposed paternalism.

B. The Popular Content

Since the lot of the individual is indissolubly linked with that of society, democracy cannot be restricted to individual freedom but should be the collective expression of the people's responsibility. The tasks of the Algerian democratic revolution are stupendous; no single social class can undertake [independently] the realization of these tasks, no matter how high its intellectual enlightenment. Only the people can fulfill these tasks—and by the people we mean the peasants, workers, tenants, and the educated revolutionary youth.

The example of certain countries which had recently become independent has shown us that a social class with special interests can seize power and rule in its own, not the people's, interest, allying itself with imperialism. The bourgeoisie claims that it works in the interest of the people and demands that the people should support it. . . .

C. The Enlightened Vanguard

To realize the goals of the people's democratic revolution it is necessary to have an enlightened vanguard. This vanguard will include the awakened elements of the peasants, workers, tenant groups, and the educated revolutionary youth. This vanguard will play an important role in formulating social and political doctrines that will truly express the aspirations of the masses. . . .

(1) Construction of a modern state and organization of the revolutionary society require the scientific approach and application of scientific methods in theory and practice. The meaning of political responsibility and performance of political duty must be

based on the objective analysis of events and sound understanding of the concrete situation. . . .

(2) This is of course impossible without rejecting all forms of subjective thought—improvisation, the approximate view of things, intellectual totalitarianism, and the idealism that dwells only on grandiose and empty events. One must, moreover, be careful not to trust the preachings of the naive idealists who want to transform society and solve its problems by means of ethical values alone. This is a false and misleading approach. The moralistic idealism which some proclaim is nothing but the cloak which hides inability to cope with social reality and to control it positively.

Revolutionary action does not consist of good intentions, however sincere these intentions may be; it must employ objective means. Individual morality, though its values may be valid and worthy in themselves, is neither essential nor decisive in the process of rebuilding society. It is rather social progress that provides the climate for social prosperity.

D. A New Definition of National Culture

Algerian culture shall be nationalist, revolutionary, and scientific.

(1) The role of nationalism in culture is represented primarily in our effort to regain for the Arabic language—the medium through which the values of our culture are best expressed—its place of honor and effectiveness as a classical culture and our humanistic tradition, both ancient and modern, and rechannel them into our cultural life. . . . We shall combat the prevailing trends, based as they are on distorted concepts of bourgeois internationalism of Western origin, which have made so many Algerians despise their own language and doubt their own national worth.

(2) Revolutionary education will play a major part in the intellectual liberation of the people by stamping out the residue of feudalism and superstition, and by conquering the old reactionary way of thinking. . . . Culture will not be the property of a privileged class, nor will it be a form of intellectual luxury. . . .

(3) Algerian culture must be scientific in its goals and methods. . . . As such it must be the vital link between the ideology of the democratic people's revolution and the practical daily tasks of rebuilding the country. . . .

ISLAM

Ours is the culture of Islam, which has made such a deep imprint on the history of man. We do harm to this culture when we believe that it is merely religious, consisting of certain modes of behavior and of religious traditions and rites. . . .

In our view Islam, after it has been cleansed of the superstitions and innovations which have long stifled it and concealed its true essence, must be embodied in two things besides religion: education and personal life. . . .

The Algerian personality will gain strength and in time become more firmly rooted, for our people are capable of moving forward with history without severing their ties with the past. . . .

No. 11 The National Charter of the United Arab Republic (Egypt)

The Charter was presented for the approval of the National Congress of Popular Forces on May 21, 1962, and was approved by acclamation on June 30, 1962. It represents the official formulation of "Arab Socialism" and sets the basis for the new socialist order in Egypt. It is meant to be an historic document, marking a major turning-point in the political and social development of the Arab world. The following excerpts are from the official translation of al-mithaq: qaddamahu al-ra'is Jamal 'Abdul-Nasser lil-mu'tamar al-watani lil-qiwa al-sha'biyyah (*Cairo: May 21, 1962*). *For a resumé of the official English translation see Alan W. Horton,* The Charter for National Action of the UAR (*American Universities Field Staff, North Africa Series, Vol. IX, No. 5*).

TRUE DEMOCRACY

True revolutionary action is impossible without popularity and progressiveness. Democracy shows that a revolution is popular; socialism shows that a revolution is progressive. Socialism means the construction of a society based on sufficiency and justice, on work and equal opportunity for all, and on production and services —thus both democracy and socialism are extensions of revolutionary action. Democracy is political freedom, and socialism is social freedom; both are indispensable to true freedom. . . .

Before the Revolution the country was dominated by an alliance of feudalism and exploiting capitalism and was a sham democracy that was really a reactionary dictatorship. The lack of social freedom led to the loss of political freedom. Without the freedom to earn a living, the freedom to vote lost all value:

1. In the villages, the peasant had to vote as the landowner instructed—or face expulsion from his land.
2. In the villages and cities, votes were easily purchased by exploiting capitalists.
3. In the villages and towns, election results could be easily forged.
4. Everywhere, the imposition of ignorance on the masses made manipulation easy.

Nor was there, before the Revolution, freedom to organize. With the loss of freedom of the press there was no longer the freedom to criticize—the press became a matter of capital investment in machinery and paper and was converted from an opportunity for expression of opinion to an instrument of the ruling group. Nor was there freedom of education: successive generations were taught that their country was incapable of industrialization, educational institutions turned out nothing more than civil servants, and intellectuals were faced with the choice of soul-destroying class privileges or obscurity.

True democracy can be outlined as follows:

1. Political democracy cannot be separated from social democracy. Nobody can be regarded as free to vote without three guarantees: freedom from exploitation in all its forms; equal opportunity for a fair share of the national wealth; and freedom from all anxiety concerning future security.
2. Political democracy cannot exist under the domination of any one class. Class strife always exists in some measure, but peaceful solutions are possible within the framework of national unity. Democratic interaction between the various working forces (namely, peasants, workers, soldiers, intellectuals, and national capital) is alone capable of replacing reactionary democracy by true democracy.
3. Cooperation between the representative working forces creates a national unity that makes possible the Arab Socialist Union—which will constitute the ultimate authority, the driving force, and

the guardian of the Revolution. The new constitution must guarantee that popular forces find expression in the following ways:

(a) Popular and political organizations based on free and direct elections must truly represent the popular forces. Peasants and workers must fill half the seats in political and popular organizations at all levels—including the Representative Assembly.

(b) The authority of elected popular councils must always be raised above the authority of the executive machinery of the state—at all levels.

(c) A new political organization, within the framework of the Arab Socialist Union, must recruit leaders and organize their efforts, clarify the revolutionary aspirations of the masses, and endeavor to satisfy the needs of the masses.

(d) Collective leadership must guard against the possible excesses of the individual and ensure the reign of true democracy.

4. Popular organizations, especially cooperatives and trade unions, can play an effective and influential role in promoting true democracy. These organizations are now free to form a vanguard of national democratic action. And it is now time that agricultural labor unions were established.

5. Criticism and self-criticism are important guarantees of freedom. The greatest obstacle to effective criticism is the infiltration of reactionary elements into political organizations. By eliminating reactionary influences, the people ensure not only effective political action but also a free press (which now belongs to the people).

6. Revolutionary conceptions of true democracy must contribute decisively to the formation of citizens—especially with respect to education and administrative regulations. Educational curricula should enable the individual to reshape his life; laws should be redrafted to fit a new situation, and justice should cease to be an expensive commodity.

THE INEVITABILITY OF THE SOCIALIST SOLUTION

Socialism is the way to social freedom; social freedom means equal opportunity to every citizen to obtain a fair share of the national wealth. The national wealth must be not only redistributed but also, and equally importantly, expanded.

The socialist solution to the problems of social and economic underdevelopment is an historical inevitability. Attempts at capitalist solutions have failed to achieve progress. Because of the development of capitalist monopolies in the advanced countries, local capitalism cannot compete without customs protection paid for by the masses and without making itself an appendage to world capitalism. The widening gap between the underdeveloped and the advanced states no longer permits that progress should be left to desultory individual efforts sustained only by the profit motive. Individual efforts cannot meet the three requirements of progress:

1. Assembling of the national savings.
2. Use of all experiences of modern science for the efficient exploitation of national savings.
3. Drafting of an over-all plan for production. Expansion and redistribution of the natural wealth cannot be left to private, voluntary efforts—hence the necessity of people's control over all the tools of production and over the disposition of surplus in accordance with scientific planning.

But control over all the tools of production does not mean the nationalization of all the means of production, the abolition of private ownership, or interference with the rights of inheritance. Control can be achieved in two ways:

1. Creation of an efficient public sector that can provide leadership for economic progress and bear the main responsibility for planned development.
2. Existence of a private sector that without unfair exploitation can contribute its share to national development within the planned framework for economic progress. . . .

CONCERNING PRODUCTION AND SOCIETY

Production is the true test of dynamic Arab power. By production we can end our underdevelopment, move rapidly toward progress, face and overcome difficulties and intrigues, and finally achieve victory over all enemies.

The battle of production, the battle to double the national income every ten years, is threatened chiefly by the increase in population. Family planning on scientific lines is necessary. Also necessary is a tremendous will to work and to produce—within the framework of a new society based on new values.

In the agricultural sector, Arab socialism does not believe in the nationalization of land but in individual ownership within limits that prevent feudalism. It believes also in agricultural cooperation in terms of credit, use of modern machinery, and marketing. The production battle in the rural areas has a threefold focus:

1. The horizontal extension of agriculture—the reclamation of desert and wasteland and the use of every drop of Nile water for irrigation.
2. The vertical extension of agriculture—the increase in productivity of land already under cultivation by means of increased application of scientific methods.
3. The industrialization and mechanization of agriculture.

Simultaneously, village life and mentality must be changed in a revolutionary and decisive way.

In the industrial sector, the latest scientific achievements and the newest equipment must compensate for present underdevelopment. Our natural and mineral wealth must be further explored. Raw materials must be processed in Egypt. Consumer industries must be further developed, not only to save foreign currency but also to earn foreign currency by export. For social reasons, heavy industry must be kept in balance with consumer industries. The workman now has a minimum wage and a seven-hour working day; he must respond to these new rights and privileges by a corresponding increase in his duties—particularly his responsibility to produce. Labor unions can now take on increased responsibilities as well.

The basis of the drive toward increased production in both agriculture and industry is an increase in motivation and the establishment of the fundamental structure basic to production. Revolutionary motivation supplies the spark for improvement in all spheres. Efficient communications networks can perform miracles in terms of the unity and organization of production.

One role of the private sector (i.e., of nonexploiting national capital) is to render public ownership more effective by providing an invigorating competitive element. The socialist laws of July 1961 did not seek to destroy the private sector but sought to:

1. Create greater economic equality among citizens and contribute to the dissolution of class distinctions.

2. Increase the efficiency of the public sector, consolidate its capacity to shoulder the responsibility of planning, and enable it to play its leading role in socialist industrial development.

The private sector is limited only by the socialist laws now in force (or by those deemed necessary by popular authorities elected in the future) and is free, within the socialist framework, to promote economic development and to make reasonable nonexploiting profits.

Foreign aid, regardless of source, is accepted in order of priority as follows: (1) unconditional aid; (2) unconditional loans; and (3) foreign investment for limited periods and unavoidable circumstances requiring international experience. Foreign aid may be viewed as an optional tax on those states with a colonial past, a compensation to the peoples who were exploited for so long.

The object of production is to provide services to society. As production and national investment increase, greater equality of opportunity is offered to the citizen. The citizen's basic rights are:

1. The right to good medical care. Health insurance must be held by each citizen.

2. The right to education that suits abilities and talents.

3. The right to secure the job that suits educational background, abilities, and interests. There should be both a minimum wage and a maximum income.

4. The right to security and rest in the event of old age or sickness.

Women must be regarded as equal to men. The family unit is basic to society and must be fostered.

The freedom of religious belief must be regarded as sacred in our new national culture with its new values. The only danger arises from reactionary attempts to exploit religion, but all religions contain a message of progress and bestow on the individual unlimited capacity for serving truth, goodness, and love.

For the individual, freedom is the greatest stimulus to all good exertion and is the basis of faith—which without freedom would become fanaticism. The individual must be free to shape his destiny, determine his position in society, express his opinion, and take an active part in his society's evolution. Law must be subservient to freedom. But no individual can be free unless he is saved from exploitation—hence, social freedom is the only way to political freedom.

Freedom of speech is the foundation of democracy; the prevalence of law is its final guarantee.

The new society, which is now being built on the basis of sufficiency and justice, needs the armed forces as a shield to defend the reconstruction of Egyptian society against external dangers. A strong army is a necessity, but the needs of defense should never have precedence over the needs of development—because without economic and social development no army can withstand the strain of long campaigns.

CONCERNING THE APPLICATION OF SOCIALISM AND ITS PROBLEMS

Creative human labor is the only means for our society to achieve its aims. Labor is an honor, a right, and a duty. The time has passed when a country could achieve its goals by other means, such as colonialist exploitation or slavery. The dignity of labor must never be threatened. Organized national labor, or action, based on scientific planning, is the way to the desired future.

National action based on planning seeks quantity and quality in a production process that stresses the importance of time and costs. All must play their roles in the national scheme based on our own and other experience. In this respect the importance of the written word cannot be overstressed—it provides the link between thought and experience and the link to our modern future.

Periods of great change are inherently full of dangers. The greatest insurance against such dangers lies in the exercise of freedom—particularly through elected popular councils which should have authority over all production centers and over the machinery of local and central administrations.

The exercise of criticism and self-criticism gives all national action an opportunity to correct its positions and to adjust to its final objectives. If popular leaders allow truth to be hidden or ignored, they fail in their duty toward those who placed leadership in their hands and they isolate themselves from the problems of the masses. The exercise of freedom not only puts an end to passivity and encourages work and sacrifice for national objectives; it also requires that popular leadership refer continually to the popular base whose willingness to work for national objectives constitutes the source of power.

The future demands hard work and holds many difficulties. The masses should not be deceived by short-term hopes; they must rally themselves to national action for the sake of a distant future.

Intellectual adolescence constitutes a danger to progress, which cannot be achieved by way of high-sounding slogans or by way of those who minimize the strength of Egyptian society in proportion to their own weakness and incapacity for creative thought.

The country's leadership must be assisted by the people but on certain occasions must be protected against itself. Leaders may wrongly assume that the great problems of national development can be solved by the complicated procedures of bureaucracy and administration. This could lead to a class of leaders isolated from public service, interested in special privileges, and convinced that the machinery of the state is an end in itself. If leaders struggle for power among themselves, moreover, power goes into fewer hands and is less responsive to the aspirations of the people. . . .

ARAB UNITY

A rallying of the popular and progressive elements on the one hand and of the reactionary and opportunistic elements on the other has taken place in every corner of the Arab world. This means that the same social currents are sweeping the area and indicates unity rather than dissension. The concept of Arab unity no longer needs bolstering by meetings of heads of state; despite the old-fashioned objectives of some Arab rulers, a popular base in each Arab country is progressive and demonstrates a unity of objective that foretells a social revolution throughout the Arab world. Imperialist forces, now unable to show their designs publicly, control matters through the reactionary palaces of some Arab nations; it is incumbent upon the Arab people to revolt against this alliance of imperialism and reaction and to consolidate the Arab right to a better social life.

Arab unity cannot be imposed. Unity must be based on the popular will and on governments representing that will. An Arab government that expresses the popular will sees no contradiction between itself and Arab unity—but the stages of development of the popular will are several, and the speeding up of those stages in some Arab states could, as experience has shown, create economic and social loopholes that could be exploited by those opposed to unity. And practical steps must be taken to fill the economic and social gaps occurring between various Arab states as a result of imperialist-inspired differences in stages of development.

The UAR must propagate her call for Arab unity and the principles it embodies—without any hesitation by reason of the outworn argument that this would be an interference in the affairs of others. Though the UAR must be careful not to involve itself in the local party disputes of any Arab state and must place the call for unity at the highest level, the UAR has a duty, nevertheless, to support and cooperate with all popular progressive movements —leaving the maneuvers of the struggle to local elements, who can act in conformity with local processes of development and change.

The Arab League, which is a league of governments, cannot go beyond the possible. It can lead Arab unity only a few steps forward and can coordinate certain aspects of Arab activity at the present stage. It deserves every support. But it should never become a means of freezing the *status quo* and thereby undermining the unity of the future. . . .

No. 12 Resolutions of the Sixth National Conference of the Ba'th Party

The conference took place on October 5, 1963, with the Ba'th party in power in both Syria and Iraq. The resolutions represent the official position of the party on socialism, Arab unity, and foreign and national policy. In November of the same year Ba'th leadership was overthrown in Iraq, and the proposed Syrian-Iraqi union consequently failed to materialize. Text in al-Nahar *(Beirut: October 29, 1963).*

1. The conference discussed the organizational problems of the party and reaffirmed the importance of keeping the principle of collective leadership inasmuch as it reflects the party's democratic spirit at the top. In light of the party's past experience, which has proven the soundness of the principle of democratic centraliza-

tion, it was decided to maintain the balance between centralization and democracy, which alone provides the opportunity for effectiveness and responsibility in the party's struggle. . . .

2. After a comprehensive study of the party in both Syria and Iraq . . . it was decided that its socialist principles should be embodied in its structure; the workers and the peasants must be the backbone and base of the socialist revolution and the party alike.

3. Given the circumstances in which the party finds itself in power in Syria and Iraq, it was deemed necessary to warn against the infiltration of opportunists into positions of authority. . . .

Emphasis was put on the necessity of close examination of the character of those applying for membership in the party, and for restriction of admissions. . . .

4. The conference approved the complete separation between party and state. It cautioned against the party becoming absorbed by government and losing itself in the daily routine of administration. It was agreed that the party should take charge of government, control major policies, and be responsible for supervising administration.

. . . . .

6. The process of socialization in Syria and Iraq is to continue on a democratic basis and in cooperation with the masses. . . . It was affirmed that the mass basis for the democratic and revolutionary experiment in the two regions would not only reflect the revolution in Syria and Iraq but would also generate repercussions in all the countries of the Arab homeland. . . .

7. After scientific analysis of the political and economic conditions in the two regions [Syria and Iraq], a number of conclusions were reached regarding the [role] of the bourgeoisie. This social and economic class is no longer capable of playing a positive part in economic life: [politically] it is an opportunistic class and constitutes a natural ally of neo-imperialism. It was declared that the socialist revolution in its first stages should be accomplished by the workers, peasants, the educated revolutionaries (military and civilian), and the small bourgeoisie.

. . . . .

9. On the problem of land [reform] it was decided that the agricultural revolution constitutes an indispensable step toward the growth of industry. Therefore the establishment of collective farms run by the farmers themselves . . . constitutes one of the primary revolutionary goals of the party. The active participation of the peasants in carrying out the agricultural revolution is an essential condition for its success.

. . . . .

12. The conference discussed the experiment of the National Guard and decided that despite certain shortcomings and mistakes, the National Guard represents a bulwark of the revolution and as such should be strengthened and expanded. . . . The conference affirmed the freedom of workers, students, professional people, and women to organize in movements and unions, provided that they remain within the broad compass of the socialist and nationalist revolution.

13. Special attention was given to ideological education in the armed forces. The full right of the military to practice its political rights was affirmed. . . .

14. After Egypt's withdrawal from the proposed unity plan [including Syria, Egypt, and Iraq], the party deemed it essential that Syria and Iraq proceed to establish the proposed union, and on this basis the conference approved the principle of unity between the Syrian and Iraqi regions. . . . The conference acknowledged the fact that the greatest step toward [greater Arab] unity would be Egypt's decision to join the new unitary state on a basis of equality among the various regions and according to the principle of collective leadership. . . .

15. The conference voted its full support for the revolutionary government of Algeria. The Algerian revolution expresses revolutionary socialism and Arab nationalism and as such constitutes a guarantee for the victory of the unitary socialist revolution throughout the Arab homeland. . . .

16. The conference denounced the persecution [by the Moroccan government] of the Socialist Union of Popular Forces, to which the party pledged its support. . . .

17. The conference studied the situation in Yemen. The Yemeni revolution was seen as another aspect of the conflict between forces

of reaction on the one hand and the masses of the people on the other. The revolution in Yemen constitutes a springboard for revolutionary action to liberate South Arabia from imperialism and the entire Arabian peninsula from reaction and the agents of imperialism. . . .

19. The conference carefully studied 'Abdul-Nasser's regime in Egypt. . . . Its positive aspects induce the party to accept the principle of unity with Egypt; but its negative aspects require that 'Abdul-Nasser be received only as a partner [in the union], so that the union will not be based on the same principles as his regime. . . . It was 'Abdul-Nasser who forced upon the party a struggle which, from the party's standpoint, has no cause other than 'Abdul-Nasser's dictatorial tendencies.

In light of present circumstances in the Arab world this conflict [with Egypt] must be brought to an end. A point of common agreement and understanding should be found to unite all the movements of liberation in the Arab homeland.

20. The conference gave special attention to the Arab problem in Palestine. It was decided that the primary means for the liberation of Palestine should be in the hands of the Palestine Arabs themselves. The idea of establishing the Palestine Liberation Front was approved. . . . An appeal was made to all the Arab states, and particularly to the revolutionary leadership of Syria and Iraq, to provide all possible assistance in establishing and organizing the Front on a revolutionary basis, and to protect it from inter-Arab conflicts.

. . . . .

22. The conference scrutinized the various forms of alliance between the bourgeois class and neo-imperialism. . . . It warned against the illusion that a socialist society with the welfare of the masses as its highest goal could be built without continuous struggle against imperialism and other forms of exploitation.

23. The conference approved the policy of nonalignment in the world struggle. . . .

24. It was made clear, however, that nonalignment should not prevent strengthening ties of friendship with the socialist countries of the world.

25. The conference confirmed the need for solidarity with the

countries of the "Third World," which pursue the positive neutrality. This solidarity will strengthen the anti-imperialist front.

26. The conference voted against racial discrimination anywhere in the world and put it in the same category as capitalist imperialism. . . .

III. Constitutional Structures*

No. 13 The Republic of Lebanon

Constitution promulgated on May 23, 1926, as amended by the constitutional laws of October 17, 1927, May 8, 1929, November 9 and December 7, 1943, and January 21, 1947; official translation, Embassy of the Republic of Lebanon, Washington, D.C.

RIGHTS

All Lebanese shall be equal in the eyes of the law. . . .

Personal freedom shall be guaranteed and protected. No Person may be arrested or kept in custody except in accordance with the law. . . .

There shall be complete freedom of conscience. While acknowledging the Most High, the Government shall respect all creeds and safeguard and protect the free exercise of all forms of worship on condition that public order is not interfered with. It shall also guarantee that the personal status and religious interests of the people, to whatever creed they may belong, shall be respected. . . .

The religious communities shall be entitled to maintain their own schools, provided that they conform to the general requirements relating to public instruction laid down by the state. . . .

All forms of public employment shall also be open to all Lebanese citizens in accordance with the conditions laid down by the law, preference being given solely to merit and capacity . . . (Articles 7, 8, 9, 10, 12).

THE POWERS

The legislative power shall be exercised by a single assembly: the Chamber of Deputies.

* For the provisional Constitutions of Syria, Iraq, and Yemen, see readings No. 28, 36, and 42, respectively.

The executive power shall be entrusted to the President of the Republic, by whom it shall be exercised with the assistance of Ministers . . . (Articles 16, 17).

CHAMBER AND PRESIDENT

Every Lebanese citizen who has completed his twenty-first year and fulfils the conditions laid down by the electoral law shall be an elector.

The Chamber of Deputies shall consist of elected members. Their number and the manner of election shall be determined by the electoral laws in force. . . .

The Chamber of Deputies shall elect the President of the Republic by secret ballot and by a two-thirds majority of the votes. . . . The President shall be elected for a term of six years. He may be reelected only after an interval of six years . . . (Articles 21, 24, 49).

CONSTITUTIONAL REVISION

The Constitution may be revised on the initiative of the President of the Republic. . . . [It] may likewise be revised on the initiative of the Chamber of Deputies . . . (Articles 76, 77).

No. 14 The Republic of Tunisia

Constitution promulgated June 1, 1959; English translation, Middle East Journal, *Vol. XIII, No. 4 (Autumn, 1959), pp. 443-448.*

GENERAL PROVISIONS

Tunisia is a free, independent and sovereign state. Its religion is Islam, and Arabic its language. Its form of government is republican.

The Republic of Tunisia is a part of the Greater Maghrib, for the unity of which she strives within the framework of common interest (Articles 1, 2).

PROPERTY

The right to property is guaranteed. It is exercised within the limits of the law (Article 14).

THE NATIONAL ASSEMBLY, PRESIDENT, AND JUDICIARY

The people exercise their legislative power through a representative assembly, the "National Assembly." . . .

The National Assembly and the President of the Republic are elected simultaneously for [a term of] five years. . . .

The President of the Republic is the Chief of State. His religion is Islam. . . .

[He] is elected for a term of five years by universal, free, direct, and secret suffrage. . . . [He] is not eligible for reelection for more than three consecutive terms. . . . [He] appoints the members of the cabinet, who are responsible to him. . . .

Judicial authority is independent: in the exercise of their functions the judges are subject to no authority save that of the law. (Articles 18, 22, 37, 40, 43, 53)

CONSTITUTIONAL REVISION

The President of the Republic or one-third at least of the members of the National Assembly may propose the amendment of the Constitution, provided that such amendment would not violate the republican form of government. (Article 60)

No. 15 The Hashemite Kingdom of Jordan

Constitution promulgated January 1, 1952, with amendments for 1954 and 1955; English translation by M. F. Abcaribus in Khalil, *Vol. I, pp. 55-75.*

THE STATE AND THE FORM OF GOVERNMENT

The Hashemite Kingdom of Jordan is an independent and sovereign Arab State. Its territory is indivisible and no portion of it may be ceded. The Jordanian people are a part of the Arab Nation and the Government of the Country is a hereditary Monarchy, parliamentary in form.

Islam is the religion of the State and Arabic its official language. . . . (Articles 1, 2)

BASIC RIGHTS

The State guarantees work and education within the limits of its possibilities. It also guarantees security and equal opportunity to all Jordanians. . . .

No property may be expropriated except for public utility and for a just compensation as provided by law. . . .

Citizens may form societies and political parties provided that their objects are lawful, their means are peaceful, and their rules do not infringe the Constitution. . . .

Elementary education is compulsory for all citizens and is free in Government schools.

The State protects labor and shall enact legislation on the following principles:

(a) The payment of a wage commensurate with the work of the laborer and its nature.

(b) Fixing the weekly hours of labor, and allowing laborers weekly and annual days of rest with pay.

(c) Determination of special compensation for laborers with families in cases of dismissal, illness, old age, and accidents arising from their work. . . . (Articles 6, 11, 16, 20, 23)

THE POWERS

The Legislative authority is vested in the King and the National Assembly, consisting of the Senate and the Chamber of Deputies.

The Executive Authority is vested in the King. He shall exercise his powers through his Ministers in accordance with the provisions of this Constitution.

The Judicial Authority is exercised by the various courts, and all judgments shall be rendered in accordance with the law and pronounced in the name of the King. (Articles 25, 26, 27)

THE KING AND HIS MINISTERS

The Throne of the Hashemite Kingdom of the Jordan is hereditary in the family of King Abdullah Ibn al-Hussein and shall devolve on his male heirs in direct line. . . . The King approves and promulgates laws. . . . He is the Commander-in-Chief of the Navy, Army, and Air Force. . . . He issues orders for the holding of elections to the Chamber of Deputies . . . [and he] dissolves the Chamber of Deputies. He appoints, dismisses, and accepts the resignation of the Prime Minister. . . .

The Prime Minister and the Ministers are collectively responsible to the Chamber of Deputies for the general policy of the State. . . . (Articles 28, 32, 34, 35, 51)

THE NATIONAL ASSEMBLY

The National Assembly shall consist of two bodies: the Senate and the Chamber of Deputies. . . .

The term of membership in the Senate is eight years. One-half of the members shall be appointed [by the King] every four years. . . .

The Chamber of Deputies shall consist of members elected by universal, secret, and direct suffrage . . . [for] a term of four years. . . . (Articles 62, 65, 67, 68)

EMERGENCY LAW

In case of serious emergency . . . the King may, on a resolution taken by the Council of Ministers, declare by Royal *Iradah* martial law in the whole or any part of the realm. When martial law is declared, the King may, by Royal *Iradah,* issue any instructions deemed necessary for the purpose of defense of the country, notwithstanding the provisions of any law in force. . . .

CONSTITUTIONAL REVISION

The procedure laid down in the Constitution for the initiation of a law shall apply to the initiation of any project purporting the amendment of the Constitution, provided that the proposal is voted for by a majority of two-thirds of the members of the Senate and of the Chamber of Deputies. . . . The proposal shall remain ineffective until it is approved by the King.

It shall not be lawful to amend the Constitution in respect of the King's prerogatives or the devolution of the Crown during a Regency. . . . (Articles 124, 126)

No. 16 The Kingdom of Morocco

Constitution approved by referendum, December 7, 1962; English translation, Embassy of Morocco, Washington, D.C.; for official French translation with English Summary, Middle East Journal, *Vol. XV, No. 3 (Summer 1961), pp. 326-328.*

GENERAL PROVISIONS

The Kingdom of Morocco, a sovereign state whose official language is Arabic, constitutes part of the Greater Maghrib.

As an African state, it has among its objectives the realization of African unity. . . . (Preamble)

Although political parties shall participate in the organization and representation of the citizens, there shall be no single-party regime in Morocco. (Article 4)

Islam shall be the official religion [of the state]. . . . (Article 6)

The right to strike shall be guaranteed. . . . The right to own property shall be guaranteed. . . . There shall be no expropriation except when pronounced by law. (Articles 14, 15)

THE KING

The King, *"Amir al-Mu'minin"* (Commander of the Faithful), shall be the symbol of the unity of the country and the guarantor of the perpetuation of the state, protector of the Faith and the Constitution. . . .

The Moroccan Crown and the constitutional rights thereof shall be inherited in direct male line and by order of primogeniture among the offspring of H. M. Hassan II. . . .

The personality of the King shall be sacred and inviolable. . . .

The King shall appoint the Prime Minister and the Cabinet members. He shall terminate their services either on his own initiative or because of their resignation, individually or in a body. The King shall preside over Cabinet meetings. . . . [He] shall have the right to dissolve the Chamber of Representatives by royal decree. . . . [He] shall preside over the Supreme Court of Justice. . . . (Articles 19, 20, 23, 24, 25, 27, 32)

PARLIAMENT

Parliament shall be composed of a Chamber of Representatives and a Chamber of Counselors. . . . Chamber of Representatives shall be elected by universal suffrage for a four-year term. . . . Two-thirds of the Chamber of Counselors shall be comprised of members elected in each town and province by an electoral college consisting of town, province, and country councils. As for the other third, it shall consist of members elected by the Chambers of Commerce, Industry, and Arts and Crafts, and by delegates from union organizations. . . .

In addition to the matters of jurisdiction referred to in other articles of the Constitution, the following shall come under the legislative power:

The individual and group rights enumerated under Chapter I of this Constitution;

The fundamental principles of the civil and criminal law;

The judicial organization of the Kingdom;

The fundamental guarantees granted to the civil and military public servants. . . . (Articles 36, 44, 45, 48)

CONSTITUTIONAL REVISION

The Prime Minister and Parliament shall alone have the right to propose a revision of the Constitution. . . . A revision shall become final after approval by referendum.

The state system of monarchy as well as the provisions made for the Islamic institutions, shall not be subject to any constitutional revision. (Articles 104, 107, 108)

No. 17 The United Kingdom of Libya

Constitution promulgated October 7, 1951: official English translation in Majid Khadduri, Modern Libya: A Study in Political Development *(Baltimore, 1963), Appendix III.*

GENERAL PROVISIONS

In the name of God the beneficent, the merciful.

We, the representatives of the people of Libya from Cyrenaica, Tripolitania, and the Fes Fezzan, meeting by the will of God in the cities of Tripoli and Benghazi in a National Constituent Assembly, having agreed and determined to form a union between us under the Crown of King Mohammed Idris el Mahdi el Senussi [Muhammad Idris al-Mahdi al-Sanussi], to whom the nation has offered the Crown and who was declared constitutional King of

Libya by this the National Constituent Assembly . . . do here prepare and resolve this Constitution for the United Kingdom of Libya. . . . (Preamble)

Islam is the religion of the State. (Article 5)

Arabic shall be the official language of the State. (Article 186)

Elementary education shall be compulsory for Libyan children of both sexes. . . . (Article 30)

Property shall be inviolable. . . . (Article 31)

THE KING

The sovereignty of the United Kingdom of Libya is vested in the nation. By the will of God the people entrust it to King Mohammed Idris el Mahdi el Senussi and after him to his male heirs, the oldest after the oldest, degree after degree. The Throne of the Kingdom is hereditary. . . . The King shall be inviolable. He shall be exempt from all responsibility.

[He] shall appoint the Prime Minister; he may remove him from office or accept his resignation. . . . (Articles 44, 45, 59, 72)

PARLIAMENT

Parliament shall consist of two chambers, the Senate and the House of Representatives.

The Senate shall consist of twenty-four members. Each of the three Provinces of the Kingdom of Libya shall have eight members.

The King appoints one-half of the members. The other members shall be elected by the legislative councils of the Provinces.

The House of Representatives shall consist of members elected in the three Provinces in accordance with the provisions of a federal electoral law. The number of deputies shall be . . . one deputy for every twenty thousand inhabitants. . . . The term of office of the members of the House of Representatives shall be four years unless it is dissolved earlier. . . . (Articles 93, 94, 100, 104)

THE PROVINCES

The Provinces shall exercise all powers which have not been assigned to the Federal Government. . . . Each Province shall formulate its own Organic Law. . . . Each Province shall have a governor who shall be called the "*Wali.*" The King shall appoint the *Wali* and may relieve him of office. The Wali shall represent the King within the Province. . . .

Each Province shall have an Executive Council [a] Legislative Council, three-quarters of the members of which at least shall be elected. (Articles 176, 177, 179, 180, 181, 182, 183)

CONSTITUTIONAL REVISION

The King or either of the two chambers may propose the revision of [the] Constitution. . . . No proposal may be made to review the provisions relating to the monarchical form of government, the order of succession to the Throne, the representative form of government, or the principles of liberty and equality, which are guaranteed by the Constitution. . . . (Articles 196, 197)

No. 18 Kuwait

Arabic text, Constitution of Kuwait (Kuwait, 1963).

FUNDAMENTAL PRINCIPLES

Kuwait is an independent Arab state enjoying complete sovereignty. . . . The people of Kuwait are part of the Arab nation. (Article 1)

Islam is the religion of the state, and the *shari'a* is a major source of legislation. . . . The official language of the state is Arabic. (Articles 2, 3)

Kuwait is a hereditary amirate in the Al Sabah family. The Crown Prince must be designated within a year after the accession of the Amir. His designation will be by nomination of the Amir and consent of the majority of the National Assembly voting in a special session. . . . (Article 4)

The form of government of Kuwait is democratic; sovereignty belongs to the nation, which is the source of all authority. Sovereignty is exercised according to the stipulations of the constitution. (Article 6)

Private property is inviolate. . . . The right to inheritance is guaranteed under the *shari'a*. . . . Confiscation of property is prohibited. . . . (Articles 18, 19)

POWERS

Legislative power rests with the Amir and the National Assembly. . . . Executive power is exercised by the Amir and the Council of Ministers. Judicial power is exercised by the courts in the name of the Amir. (Articles 51, 52, 53)

The Amir is the chief of state. . . . Upon his election his yearly expenditure is determined by law which will be effective so long as he remains in office. . . . The National Assembly is composed of fifty members elected by direct secret suffrage. . . . No authority has power over judges in exercising their duties, and it is against the law to influence in any manner the normal course of justice. . . . (Articles 54, 78, 163)

CONSTITUTIONAL REVISION

The Amir and one-third of the members of the National Assembly have the right to propose revision of the constitution. . . . (Article 174)

No. 19 The Algerian People's Democratic Republic

Constitution adopted by the Algerian National Assembly on August 28, 1963 and approved by referendum, September 8, 1963; unofficial English translation, Middle East Journal, *Vol. XVII, No. 4 (Summer 1963), pp. 446-450.*

GENERAL PRINCIPLES

Algeria is a Democratic and Popular Republic.

It is an integral part of the Arab Maghreb, of the Arab World, and of Africa.

Islam is the religion of the State.

Arabic is the national and official language of the State. . . . The French language may be used provisionally with the Arab language. (Articles 1, 2, 4, 5, 73)

OBJECTIVES

The fundamental objectives of the Democratic and Popular Republic of Algeria are:

The safeguard of the national independence, territorial unity and national unity;

The exercise of power by the people, whose vanguard are the peasants (fellahs), workers, and revolutionary intellectuals;

The construction of a socialistic democracy, the struggle against the exploitation of man in all its forms;

The elimination of all remnants of colonialism;

The defense of liberty and the absolute respect for the dignity of the human being;

The struggle against all discrimination, in particular, that based on race or religion;

World Peace.

The Republic condemns torture and all physical or moral attacks on human integrity. (Article 10)

THE FRONT OF NATIONAL LIBERATION

The FLN (Front of National Liberation) is the single party of leadership in Algeria. [It] carries out the objectives of the democratic and popular revolution and constructs socialism in Algeria. [It] reflects the profound aspirations of the masses and guides them for the achievement of these aspirations. It educates and provides leadership for the masses.

The FLN defines the policy of the Nation and inspires the action of the State. It controls the action of the National Assembly and of the Government. (Articles 56, 57, 58, 59)

THE NATIONAL ASSEMBLY

National sovereignty is vested in the people, who shall exercise it through their representatives to a National Assembly designated by the Front of National Liberation and elected for five years by direct and secret universal suffrage, according to the conditions set by law. The National Assembly expresses the popular will; it votes the law and controls governmental action. . . . [It] exercises control over governmental action by:

Appearance of Ministers before the Committees;

Written questions;

Oral questions with or without debate. (Articles 23, 24, 33)

THE PRESIDENT

The Executive Power is vested in the Chief of State, who bears the title of President of the Republic. He is elected for five years by direct and secret universal suffrage after designation by the Party. . . . [He] is alone responsible before the National Assembly. [He] names the Ministers and presents them to the Assembly. [He] conducts and coordinates the internal and external policy of the nation in conformity with the will of the people, given form through the Party and expressed by the National Assembly. . . . In case of imminent danger, the President of the Republic may take exceptional measures in view of safeguarding the independence of the Nation and the institutions of the Republic. . . . (Articles 34, 41, 42, 52)

CONSTITUTIONAL REVISION

Initiative for constitutional revision rests jointly with the President of the Republic and an absolute majority of the National Assembly. (Article 68)

No. 20 The United Arab Republic

Constitution proclaimed March 25, 1964; English translation, UAR., Information Department (*Cairo, 1964*).

GENERAL PRINCIPLES

The United Arab Republic is a democratic, socialist State based on the alliance of the working powers of the people.

The Egyptian people are part of the Arab nation.

Islam is the religion of the State and Arabic its official language. (Articles 1, 5)

ARAB SOCIALIST UNION

National unity, formed by the alliance of the people's powers, representing the working people, being the farmers, workers, soldiers, intellectuals and national capital, make up the Arab Socialist Union, as the power representative of the people, driver of the Revolution's potentialities, and protector of sound democratic values. (Article 2)

SOCIALISM

The economic foundation of the State is the socialist system. . . . The entire national economy is directed in accordance with the development plan laid down by the State.

Ownership assumes the following forms:

(a) *State Ownership,* or the ownership of the people through the creation of an able and strong public sector which leads progress in all spheres and assumes the main responsibility in the development plan.

(b) *Cooperative Ownership,* or the ownership of all the members of the cooperative society.

(c) *Private Ownership.* A private sector which takes part in the development, within the framework of its overall plan, without any exploitation. . . .

Private ownership is safeguarded and the law organizes its social function, and ownership is not expropriated except for the general good and against a fair compensation in accordance with the law. The law fixes the maximum limit of land ownership and defines the measures of protecting small land ownerships. The State guarantees social insurance services and Egyptians have the right to aid in cases of old age, sickness, incapacity to work, and unemployment. . . . (Articles 9, 10, 13, 16, 17, 20)

THE NATIONAL ASSEMBLY

The National Assembly is composed of members elected by secret public election. . . . The number of elected members, the conditions of membership . . . the method and the rules of the election are defined by law. The President of the Republic may appoint a number of members not exceeding ten. At least one-half of the members of the Assembly must be workers and farmers. . . . The duration of the National Assembly is five years from the date of its first meeting. . . .

The National Assembly exercises control over the acts of Government. The Government and its members are responsible for their acts before the National Assembly, which discusses their policy statements and reports. . . . (Articles 49, 51, 83)

THE PRESIDENT

The National Assembly nominates the President of the Republic. The nomination is referred to the people for a plebiscite. The candidate who wins two-thirds of the votes of the Assembly members is referred to the people for a plebiscite. . . . The candidate is considered President of the Republic when he obtains an absolute majority of the votes cast in the plebiscite. . . .

The term of the Presidency is six Gregorian years starting on the date of the announcement of the result of the plebiscite. . . .

The President of the Republic may appoint one or more Vice-Presidents and relieve them of their posts. . . .

The President of the Republic has the right to dissolve the National Assembly. . . .

[He,] in conjunction with the Government, lays down the general policy of the State in all the political, economic, social, and administrative domains and supervises its implementation. [He] appoints the Prime Minister and relieves him of his post. . . .

In the case of the President's resignation, permanent disability, or death, the First Vice-President temporarily assumes the Presidency. . . . (Articles 91, 102, 103, 107, 110, 113, 114)

CONSTITUTIONAL REVISION

The President of the Republic as well as the National Assembly may request a revision of one or more of the articles of the Constitution. . . . If the modification is approved by two-thirds of the members of the Assembly, it shall come into force from the date of approval. (Article 165)

No. 21 The Pact of the League of Arab States

The Pact was signed in Cairo on March 22, 1945, by the seven founding states (Egypt, Iraq, Syria, Lebanon, Transjordan, Sa'udi Arabia, and Yemen); Arabic text in Ahmad Musa, Mithaq Jami'at al-duwal al-'arabiyyah *(Cairo, 1948), pp. 1-7.*

COMPOSITION

The League of the Arab States shall be composed of the independent Arab States signatories to this Pact.

Each independent Arab State shall have the right to adhere to the League. . . . (Article I)

OBJECTIVE

The object of the League shall be to strengthen the ties between the participant states, to coordinate their political programs in such a way as to effect real collaboration between them, to preserve their independence and sovereignty, and to consider in general the affairs and interests of the Arab countries.

A further object shall be the close collaboration . . . in the following matters:

1. Economic and financial affairs, comprising trade reciprocity, tariffs, currency, agricultural, and industrial matters.
2. Communications, comprising railways, roads, aviation, navigation, posts, and telegraphs.
3. Cultural affairs.
4. Matters relating to nationality, passports and visas, execution of judgments, and extradition of criminals.
5. Matters relating to social questions.
6. Matters relating to public health. (Article II)

THE COUNCIL

The League shall have a Council to be composed of representatives of the states participant in the League. . . . The Council's functions shall be the realization of the objects of the League. . . . (Article III)

INTER-ARAB DISPUTES

Recourse to force to resolve disputes between two or more League states is inadmissible. . . . The Council shall mediate in any dispute which causes apprehension concerning a state of war between one of the League states and another. . . . Decisions of arbitration and mediation shall be issued by majority opinion. (Article V)

COUNCIL DECISIONS

Decisions of the Council by unanimous assent shall be obligatory on all the states participant in the League. Decisions of the League by majority [vote] shall be obligatory on those who accept them. . . . (Article VII)

NONINTERFERENCE IN DOMESTIC AFFAIRS

Each state participant in the League shall respect the existing regime obtaining in the other League states, regarding it as a [fundamental] right of those states, and pledges itself not to undertake any action tending to alter that regime. (Article VIII)

ADMINISTRATIVE PROVISIONS

Cairo shall be the permanent seat of the League of Arab States. . . . (Article X) The League shall have a permanent Secretariat-General, consisting of a Secretary-General, Assistant Secretaries, and an appropriate staff of officials. . . . (Article XII)

AMENDMENT OF THE PACT

It is permissible by agreement of two-thirds of the League states to amend this Pact, especially in order to render the ties between them firmer and closer, to found an Arab Court of Justice, and to coordinate the relations of the League with international organizations. . . . (Article XIX)

IV. The Coups d'État

SYRIA

Texts in Muhammad Khalil, The Arab States and the Arab League *(Beirut, 1962), Vol. I., pp. 521, 529-535, 556-559, 592-594;* Watha'iq wa dirasat [*Documents and Studies*], *Vol. VII (15 April 1963), pp. 205-206; text of provisional constitution in* al-Ba'th *(Damascus), April 28, 1964.*

No. 22 First Public Statement Following Husni al-Za'im's Coup d'État, March 30, 1949

To the Noble Syrian People:

Today a new page has been turned in the life of the Arab people of Syria; other pages have been closed. The page turned is one of heroism and glory; the closed ones are of humiliation and disgrace.

The gallant Syrian Army has been mindful of the state of anarchy, exploitation and defection into which this country has sunk. The present regime has been found to abound in vices and in disgrace, including betrayals and robberies, suppression of democratic freedom, and the violation of the constitution and laws.

The Army witnessed all this . . . it could not stand by with its arms folded. . . . It has therefore decided to take an honorable stand by intervening to put things right and to restore to this nation its honor, dignity, and freedom. . . .

This glorious coup has been accomplished without shedding a drop of blood or firing a bullet. Today, God willing, a new national democratic government will be formed in order to save the country from the horrors of the old regime, provide the people with a calm atmosphere for enjoying their constitutional liberties, and ensure for them a high and honorable standard of living that will be worthy of their true patriotism and past sacrifices.

The way is now open for the Arab people of Syria to go ahead in the realization of their eternal mission.

The General Command of the Army
and the Armed Forces

No. 23 Second Coup d'État, August 14, 1949

Free Syrians:

Praise God, the Sublime and Almighty, the real coup d'état has been accomplished, and the country has been saved from the criminal and despotic tyrant who had deviated from the proper course and who had ruled most despotically. . . .

The tyrant had said, in justification of his coup, that he had carried out [that] coup in order to save the country from the state of misery and anarchy into which it had sunk during the previous regime. But he ran the country in such a way that people began to speak well of the old regime and to wish it would return, despite its defects and shortcomings. . . .

Your army has, once more, carried out a coup d'état, and its Supreme Commander assures you that he would not have carried out his movement except to save the reputation of the country and its dignity from the [sad state] it had fallen into. Tomorrow he will invite all free men of the country, regardless of the diversity of their propensities and parties, to take over the reins of government, in the form they will choose. Then he and the Army will return to their posts in order to defend the frontiers and maintain the dignity of the country, [well] away from interference in politics, for politics has its own masters. . . .

Brigadier Sami al-Hinnawi,
Commander-in-Chief
of the Armed Forces

No. 24 Statement of the General National Congress, Condemning Shishakly's Regime, September 5, 1950

[Brigadier Shishakly had taken over from Brigadier Hinnawi shortly after the second coup.]

The striving Syrian people should know where they stand in this crisis from which the country is suffering, and should realize that their men, who are the custodians of their liberties, are still exerting efforts and remaining loyal to justice and to the fatherland.

The nationalists have been shocked and horrified at the tottering structure of this nation. . . . Until March 30, 1949, the country had enjoyed sovereignty, internal stability, an exceptional international reputation, and a highly prized and inviolable independence, which had not been the object of anyone's ambition. Since that time internal stability has been lost, our external reputation has collapsed, and [our] independence has become a prey to [foreign] ambition. . . .

The National Congress appeals to the people vigorously and boldly and promises them that it will sacrifice life, effort, and money, in order to prove that all which is founded on unlawful grounds shall be destroyed by the forces of justice and goodness. . . . It accepts no compromise concerning respect for the nation's Constitution; it is determined to preserve the dignity of the people and the sanctity of the Constitution. . . .

No. 25 Statement by Leaders and Members of Political Parties Addressed to the Chief of The General Staff (Brigadier Shishakly), June 20, 1953

. . . Our country today is being governed by individual absolute rule. It is evident that this type of rule cannot, of its very nature, admit control, does not inspire public security, and does not fulfill any meaning of the fundamental safeguards for individuals or groups. The first feature [of this type of rule] has been the complete loss of public liberties, which has subjected the citizens to a form of suppression and fostered the feelings of alienation and estrangement between the two groups in the country: the ruler and the ruled. This has resulted in a feeling among the people of the nonsupremacy of the law. They have thus come to perceive this phenomenon in a concrete form in many public and individual cases. . . .

We think it important to point out that the Constitution of the nation should not be drawn up in the departments of the government by some of its officials. No constitution of any nation has to our knowledge been drawn up in this manner. . . .

It is an established fact that in free countries there are only two ways of drawing up a constitution:

First: By the election of a constituent assembly. . . .

Second: By constitutive referendum, whereby the nation elects a constituent council that drafts, discusses, and votes on the Constitution. . . .

Hoping that this statement will be received by an attentive ear, an understanding heart, and an appreciative mind, we pray to God Almighty to bring about the welfare of this nation . . . and protect it from storms and perils that menace it in all quarters.

[Signatures]

No. 26 Statement by Captain Mustafa Hamdun on Behalf of the Aleppo Garrison Against the Shishakly Regime, February 25, 1954

. . . The Army of the people wanted a revolution in national construction and new development—revolution for the glory and freedom of the people. . . . But today, unfortunately, we find ourselves standing beside you [facing the wreckage] of two and a half years of dismal rule, and great is our grief when we see nothing but tears. . . .

Shishakly claimed, in justification of his seizure of power, that he wanted his movement to realize the people's demands and to protect the country against foreign plots, to set up a republican, democratic, popular and free regime.

The result was that he waged a cruel war against the people . . . dissolved the political parties, arrested their leaders . . . confiscated their property . . . monopolized political acts . . . [and] barbarously shed the blood of tens of men and women students. . . .

We declare, in the name of the whole people, and in that of the officers of Aleppo, Hama, Homs, Dayr al-Zur and Latakia, that al-Shishakly is a criminal oppressor who should immediately accede to the will of the people by relinquishing power and leaving the country. . . . We call upon the people to exercise their powers alone, effectively and honestly, to set up their own republican popular regime, and to [help] the Army to return to its ideal duty of protecting the fatherland and maintaining its safety.

[Signature]

No. 27 First Statement Following the Ba'th Coup d'État, March 8, 1963

Since the dawn of Arab awakening, Syria has played a positive role in the struggle for Arabism and unity. The Syrians have never accepted the present boundaries of Syria and have always lived within the boundaries of the Greater Arab fatherland. . . . When the League of Arab States was established, Syria gave it its full support, and when unity was realized between Egypt and Syria and the United Arab Republic . . . the entire Arab people of Syria rushed to bolster it with all its heart and soul. . . .

Arab people of Syria:

A year and a half have passed since the secession, which has been the most difficult period you have experienced—elections in favor of the exploiters supervised by imperialism and reaction, a prejudiced press which expressed none of your feelings and beliefs but trampled upon your aspirations and hopes, and an isolation from the liberated countries which increased day after day. . . .

The army coup has as its goal putting the army on the right course again. The army and the people have an unshakeable belief in Arab unity based on sound foundations.

The army will honor its international agreements and obligations, and will continue to adhere to the United Nations Charter, the resolutions of the Bandung Conference, and the principles of positive neutrality and international cooperation on the basis of mutual respect and equality.

The army supports the Yemeni revolution . . . and backs the revolution in Iraq. . . . Arab Syria extends her hand [in friendship] to Baghdad, Cairo, Sana, and Algiers, and to all freedom fighters everywhere.

We resolve before God to follow the right path leading to the prosperity of our Arab nation, which is struggling to achieve unity, freedom, and socialism. God is Great and Glory to the Arabs.

No. 28 Ba'th Provisional Constitution, April 27, 1964

SYRIAN ARAB REPUBLIC

The Syrian region is a sovereign democratic people's socialist republic and part of the Arab fatherland. The Arab people of Syria are part of the Arab nation. They believe in [Arab] unity and struggle for its realization.

The religion of the head of state is Islam. Muslim jurisprudence is the principal source of legislation. . . . (Articles 1, 2)

OWNERSHIP, PRODUCTION, AND INHERITANCE

The state shall place all the country's wealth and resources in the service of the people under a plan that shall prevent exploitation and promote national income, which shall be justly distributed in line with producers' efforts.

The socialist society is based on collective ownership of all means of production. The ownership of the means of production shall be as follows: (a) State ownership—represented in the public sector, shall bear the great responsibility in the development plan, and shall own public utilities, principal means of communication, and the means of production connected with the public's basic requirements. (b) Collective ownership—which is the ownership of all producers. (c) Individual ownership. Personal holdings are safeguarded. . . . [They] shall be expropriated only in the public interest. . . . The law shall define the maximum holdings permissible . . . The state shall nationalize by law every institution or project connected with public interest. . . . Inheritance right is safeguarded by law. (Articles 23, 24, 25, 26, 27, 29, 30)

THE POWERS

The National [Revolutionary] Council shall undertake the legislative power and supervise the executive authority's work. . . . The executive power shall be exercised by the Presidential Council and the Cabinet of Ministers. . . .

The National Council shall be composed of its present members and representatives of the public sector. . . . [It] shall carry out the following duties: elect the chairman, vice chairman, and members of the Presidential Council . . . draw up the state's general policy program and approve the transitional period . . . decide on matters of peace and war . . . grant or withhold confidence in the cabinet or any of the ministers.

The Presidential Council shall be composed of a chairman, vice chairman, and three members elected by the National Council from among its members. [It] shall be responsible to the National Council for all aspects of its activity. [It] shall appoint and dismiss the cabinet ministers . . . may proclaim a state of emergency and partial mobilization by decree . . . draw up domestic and foreign policy . . . appoint and dismiss civil and military officials.

The Cabinet of Ministers shall be composed of premier and ministers. . . . The premier shall be from among the members of the National Council. The Cabinet shall collectively be responsible to the National Council. . . . (Articles 31, 32, 33, 47, 48, 50, 53, 54, 55, 59, 61)

This provisional constitution shall be in force until the people approve the permanent constitution, within a period not to exceed one year as of the proclamation of this constitution. (Article 80)

EGYPT

Texts in Khalil, I, pp. 492-493; Middle Eastern Affairs, *Vol. IV, No. 3 (March 1953), p. 105; Vol. IV, Nos. 8-9 (August-September 1953), pp. 295-296.*

No. 29 First Statement Following the Coup d'État, July 23, 1952

Egypt has undergone a most critical period of bribery, corruption, and government instability in her recent history. These factors had a great influence on the Army. People who received bribes and those with ulterior motives contributed to our defeat in the

Palestine war. After the war corrupt elements increased, and traitors plotted against the Army, whose affairs were entrusted to ignorant, treacherous, or corrupt people. This was in order that Egypt would be without a strong Army to protect her.

Because of this, we have now purged ourselves, and our affairs within the Army have been entrusted to men in whose ability, character, and patriotism we have faith.

The whole of Egypt will welcome this news with rejoicing.

No injury will, however, be suffered by those former leaders of the Army whom we have seen fit to arrest, and they will be released in due course.

I [should like to] assure the Egyptian people that the entire Army is today working for the interests of the fatherland within the Constitution and without any designs of its own.

I take this opportunity to appeal to the people not to allow any traitors to resort to acts of sabotage or violence. . . .

I should like to assure foreign residents, our brothers, of the safety of their lives and property; the Army considers itself responsible for them.

May God grant us prosperity.

Major-General Muhammad Naguib,
Commander-in-Chief of the
Armed Forces

No. 30 Ultimatum to King Farouk, July 26, 1952

From Major-General Muhammad Naguib, in behalf of the officers and men of the Army, to His Majesty King Farouk the First:

Whereas widespread anarchy has of late been dominating all fields throughout the country as a result of your misconduct, your tampering with the Constitution, and your callous disregard of the will of the people, to such an extent that no individual could feel secure as to his life, his property, or his dignity;

And [whereas] your persistence in pursuing this course has compromised the reputation of Egypt in the eyes of the peoples of the world. . . .

And [whereas] a clear proof of this was demonstrated by the Palestine war, the subsequent defective arms scandals, and the trials which took place in consequence thereof and which suffered from your open interference. . . .

Therefore, the Army, representing the power of the people, has authorized me to demand that Your Majesty abdicate the throne in favor of your Crown Prince, His Highness Prince Ahmad Fu'ad, provided that this shall take place at the latest at twelve noon today, Saturday, July 26, 1952, and that you leave the country before six p.m. of the same day.

The Army will hold Your Majesty responsible for all the consequences which may follow from refusal to comply with the wishes of the people.

No. 31 Three-Year Transition Period Declared, February 10, 1953

Desiring to stabilize the system of Government during the transition period and to define the rights and obligations of citizens so that the country may enjoy complete stability . . . I declare in the name of the people that the country's rule during the transition period shall be in accordance with the following rules:

. . . . .

Article 8. The leaders of the Revolution, presiding over the Revolutionary Command Council, shall assume full sovereign powers, particularly in regard to measures deemed necessary to protect the Revolution, the system on which it is based to achieve its objectives, as well as the right to appoint and dismiss Ministers.

Article 9. The Council of Ministers shall exercise legislative powers.

Article 10. The Council of Ministers and the Ministers shall exercise executive powers, each insofar as he is concerned.

Article 11. A Congress shall be composed of the Revolution Command Council and the Council of Ministers to consider the general policy of the State and subjects connected with it, and the right to question the work of every Minister.

My Countrymen, in declaring these principles and rules, I announce in absolute faith the necessity of the establishment of a constitutional democratic regime, following the termination of the transition period, and the necessity of ensuring a free and respectable life and a bright future towards which all of us must strive.

Major-General Muhammad Naguib,
Commander-in-Chief of the
Armed Forces and Leader of
the Army Revolution

No. 32 Proclamation of the Republic, June 18, 1953

The Revolution was brought about in order to put an end to imperialism and its partisans. Furthermore, on July 26, 1952, ex-King Farouk was asked to abdicate his throne because he represented the cornerstone on which imperialism depended.

Yet since that date and since the abolition of political parties, certain elements with outmoded ideas have depended for their existence and survival upon the monarchical regime, which the whole nation was unanimous in wishing to see disappear forever. . . .

Farouk surpassed his predecessors. He enriched and perjured himself. He became a despot without conscience, thus tracing with his own hands his end and his destiny.

The moment has therefore come for the country to free itself from every trace of the servitude imposed upon it by these events. We therefore proclaim today in the name of the people the abolition of the monarchy, the end of the dynasty of Muhammad Ali, as well as that of the titles of the members of that family.

We proclaim the Republic. General Muhammad Naguib, Leader of the Revolution, becomes President of the Republic, at the same time conserving his present powers under the provisional Constitution. This Government will remain in force during the whole transitional period and the people will have the last word on the form of the Republic and the choice of the President with the promulgation of the new Constitution.

Let us have confidence in God and in ourselves. May God help us and grant us success.

[The Revolutionary Command Council]

IRAQ

Texts in Middle Eastern Affairs, *Vol. IX, Nos. 8-9* (*August-September 1958*), *p. 267;* watha'iq wa dirasat, *Vol. VI* (*April 1, 1963*), *pp. 192-195;* al-manar (*May 4 and 5, 1964*).

No. 33 Announcement of the Coup d'État, July 14, 1958

With the aid of God Almighty and the support of the people and the armed services, we have liberated the country from the domination of a corrupt group which was installed by imperialism to lull the people.

The army is yours. It has already achieved your wish and got rid of tyrants who played with the rights of the people. It is your duty to support it. Victory can be achieved only through the organization of the army and by defending it against imperialist conspiracies.

We appeal to the people to inform the authorities of all traitors and corrupt persons so that we may get rid of them. We ask you to be united in an effort to destroy those criminals and to rid the country of their evils.

We call on you to be calm and to uphold discipline, unity, and cooperation in the interests of the country.

Be confident that we shall continue to work for you. Power will be given to a government inspired by the people.

There will be an Iraqi republic which will preserve Iraqi unity, maintain brotherly ties with the other Arab countries, and fulfill all obligations and treaties which are in the interest of the country, and carry out the principles of the Bandung Conference and the United Nations Charter.

This new national government will now be called the Iraqi Republic.

A council of sovereignty will carry out presidential duties until there is a general plebiscite.

[Brigadier 'Abdul Karim Kassem]

No. 34 Counter-Coup, February 8, 1963

From the Revolutionary Command Council;

In the name of God, the Merciful, the Compassionate;

Esteemed Iraqi People:

With the help of God we have destroyed 'Abdul Karim Kassem, the enemy of the people, and his gang which has exploited the country's resources to spread its cause and realize its interests. Freedom was suppressed, dignity trampled upon, trust betrayed, laws suspended, and the people persecuted. The July 14 revolution had been executed to free our country from imperialism entrenched in the monarchical regime, to get rid of feudal domination, and to put an end to the policy of submission. [We aimed at] establishing a democracy under which the people could enjoy peace and dignity, but the treacherous criminal, God's enemy and yours, took advantage of his position and employed all criminal means to establish his black rule. . . .

Oh esteemed people:

This movement undertaken by both the people and the army [aims at] continuing the victorious course of the revolution of July 14, which must realize two goals:

First, national unity, and

Second, the people's participation in the government.

In order to realize these two goals it is imperative that public freedoms and supremacy of the law be reestablished. . . .

The [new] government shall strive to reestablish the democratic freedoms, bolster the supremacy of law, realize national unity, and strengthen the ties of Arab-Kurdish brotherhood. It shall work to safeguard national interests, strengthen the common struggle against imperialism, and strengthen respect for the rights of the minorities so that they may be better able to participate in national life. . . .

No. 35 Execution of 'Abdul Karim Kassem, March 9, 1963

Communiqué from the Military Governor:

'Abdul Karim Kassem, the enemy of the people, together with

Fadil al-Mahdawi, Taha al-Sheikh Ahmad, and Kan'an Salim Haddad, have been captured by the armed forces.

A court martial was formed to try them. They were sentenced to death by firing squad. The sentence was carried out at 1:30 this afternoon.

[Signature]

No. 36 Provisional Constitution, April 29, 1964

The Iraqi Republic is a democratic socialist state deriving the rudiments of its democracy and socialism from the Arab heritage and the spirit of Islam. The Iraqi people are a part of the Arab nation and its aim is total Arab unity. The government binds itself to achieve this unity as soon as possible, starting with unity with the UAR.

Private property is inviolable. . . . The law determines the [maximum] of agricultural ownership in such a manner as to prevent the establishment of a feudal system. . . .

The incumbent president of the republic shall continue to perform the functions of his post until a new president is elected in accordance with the provisions of the permanent constitution. The interim period shall not exceed three years from the date this transitional constitution comes into force. The president of the republic shall appoint the premier, the deputy premier, and the ministers and shall accept their resignations and relieve them of their posts. He shall have the power to declare martial law and a state of emergency with approval of the Revolutionary Command Council.

The president of the republic, in cooperation with the government, shall lay down the general policy of the state in all the military, political, economic, and social aspects and shall supervise its implementation. The cabinet shall exercise the legislative powers during the transitional period, while observing the provisions of the law of the Revolutionary Command Council. The president of the republic shall rectify the laws and promulgate them. (Articles 1, 12, 13, 43, 48, 59, 63, 100, 101)

SUDAN

Texts in Khalil, I, pp. 359-361.

No. 37 First Statement Following Coup d'État, November 17, 1958

Compatriots:

Sincere greetings to you all.

You are all well aware of the [prevailing] state of corruption, maladministration, instability, and individual and community fear, and how the evils of corruption have extended without exception to the State machinery and public utilities. All this has been due to the interparty strife from which the country has been suffering. Each [party] wanted to rule for its own ends, by every means, lawful and unlawful, and to establish relations with foreign powers and embassies. In doing so [they were] not [motivated] by the desire to safeguard the independence of the Sudan, nor by the desire to ameliorate the conditions of the needy people, but were only competing for power and dominating the State and its institutions.

We have for a long time been patient with the successive partisan governments. However, regrettably enough, conditions only deteriorated; each party tampered with the safety of the Sudan. Every citizen complained of the deterioration of conditions and of the anarchy and corruption resulting therefrom. The country was on the brink of a precipice.

As a result of this perverted conduct [by the parties], it became obvious that our duty was to put an end to all this, so that all might feel secure.

Thank God your loyal Army has, on this day, the seventeenth of November, taken this sound and blessed step, which will be the turning point from corruption to integrity and honesty. I am certain that every sincere person will welcome this revolution. . . .

As the security forces have taken over power in order to carry out reform and to put an end to corruption, I have ordered the following immediately to be put into effect:

First: Dissolution of all political parties.

Second: Banning of meetings, processions, and demonstrations in all districts.

Third: Suspension of all newspapers until a further order is issued by the Ministry of Interior. . . .

Lieutenant-General Ibrahim 'Abboud

No. 38 Proclamations

No. 1

I, Lieutenant-General Ibrahim 'Abboud,

In view of the state of maladministration, corruption, and anarchy which has pervaded the country . . .

By virtue of the powers vested in me by the Supreme Council of the Armed Forces, and by Article 2 of the Martial Administration Law,

Do hereby proclaim a state of emergency throughout the whole of the Sudan, and appoint military officers to exercise power in accordance with the law.

No. 2

I . . . declare the suspension of the Provisional Sudanese Constitution, and the dissolution of Parliament as from today, November 17, 1958, until the Supreme Council of the Armed Forces makes a decision in this regard.

No. 3

I . . . do hereby order the suspension of newspapers and news bulletins until a further order is issued by the Supreme Council of the Armed Forces.

No. 39 Constitutional Order No. 1, November 18, 1958

By virtue of the powers vested in the Supreme Council of the Armed Forces, in conformity with the statement issued by its Chief on November 17, 1958,

The Council decided, at its meeting held on November 18, 1958, to issue the following Constitutional Orders:

First: The Sudan is a democratic republic in which sovereignty belongs to the people, in whose name all laws shall be issued.

Second: The Supreme Council of the Armed Forces is [the source of] the supreme constitutional powers in the Sudan.

Third: The Supreme Council shall authorize its Chief, Lieutenant-General Ibrahim Pasha 'Abboud, to assume legislative, executive, and judicial powers, as well as to command the Armed Forces.

YEMEN

Texts in watha'iq wa dirasat, *Vol. V (March 15, 1963), pp. 180, 182-183; text of Provisional Constitution in* al-thawrah *(Baghdad), May 2, 1964.*

No. 40 First Statement by the Yemeni Revolutionary Council, September 26, 1962

The Yemeni Army, in collaboration with the Free Yemenis and the Chiefs of the tribes, has carried out a revolution in the name of God and the People. . . .

Citizens,

Hundreds of years have passed during which the people have been subjected to injustice, insult, and tyranny. The tyrants have stolen your wealth, violated your honor, and used you for their own ends.

O Arab people of Yemen,

Our revolution is an Arab nationalist revolution, in the service of the people and in the interest of the people. The Arab revolution is everywhere.

The Arab Yemeni revolution believes in Arab unity, in Arab nationalism, and in the Arab nation.

The revolution has taken place in the name of God and the people in order to realize the goals of the people, to safeguard their interests, and to realize for the people prosperity and security.

Long live the Arab people of Yemen! Long live the Arab nation!

No. 41 First Press Interview with General 'Abdullah al-Sallal, Head of the Yemeni Revolutionary Council

Our revolution aims at realizing the following goals:

First: To put an end to those things that have blocked all progress in Yemen—tyranny, reaction, corrupt government, and the evil system of monarchy.

Second: To eliminate social and political injustice, to remove the great inequalities between classes, to put an end to racial discrimination, and to safeguard the internal unity of the country.

Third: To establish an Arab Republic of Yemen which will be an inseparable part of the Greater Arab Fatherland.

Four: To create a sound national army capable of defending the Arab Republic of Yemen against its enemies both within and without, and of participating in the liberation of Palestine and of all the Arabs still struggling to achieve freedom.

Five: To build a truly free republic in Yemen.

[Middle East News Agency]

No. 42 Provisional Constitution, April 28, 1964

Yemen is a sovereign, independent, Arab, Islamic state. It is a democratic republic. The people of Yemen are part of the Arab nation. Islam is the religion of the state, and Arabic is its official language. Islamic jurisprudence shall be the source of all legislation.

Private ownership is inviolable. . . . Freedom of opinion and of scientific research is guaranteed. . . .

The formation of trade unions is a guaranteed right. . . .

Observation of public discipline and respect for Islamic ethics is a duty imposed on all Yemenis.

The citizens shall form a popular organization to work for the realization of the aims of the revolution and to consolidate their efforts to build the country on a sound basis.

The Consultative Assembly is the body which exercises the legislative power. [It] shall be formed of members selected from among the people of Yemen and Yemeni wisemen. The law shall define the number of members, conditions for membership, manner, and rules of appointment. . . . The president may dissolve the Consultative Assembly. . . .

The Consultative Assembly shall nominate the president of the republic . . . the term for the presidency is five years. . . .

The president of the republic, in collaboration with the government, shall lay down the general policy of the state in all political, economic, social, and administrative aspects, and shall supervise its implementation. He shall appoint the premier and shall relieve him of his post. . . . The term of the present president shall begin from the date he takes the oath in the presence of the Consultative Assembly.

Judges shall be independent. In the administration of justice they shall be subject to no other authority save that of Islamic law. No power may interfere in lawsuits or in the affairs of justice. (Articles 1, 3, 4, 5, 33, 39, 43, 46, 48, 87, 94, 95, 104, 141, 154, 155)

Selected Readings and References

ESSENTIAL READINGS

The following five works are indispensible for any proper understanding of the modern Arab world: Bernard Lewis, *The Arabs in History* (New York, 1951), the best and most concise analysis of the rise and flowering of Arab civilization; H. A. R. Gibb, *Modern Trends in Islam* (Chicago, 1947), the standard authoritative treatment; George Antonius, *The Arab Awakening* (Philadelphia, 1938), the classic work on the rise of Arab nationalism; Jacques Berque, *Les Arabes d'hier à demain* (Paris, 1960), a profound sociological study of the contemporary Arab scene in North Africa and the Middle East; and Albert Hourani, *Arabic Thought in the Liberal Age, 1798-1939* (London, 1962), the definitive work on Arab intellectual history.

GENERAL WORKS

Morroe Berger, *The Arab World Today* (New York, 1962), provides a good introduction to the social structure of Arab society in the Middle East; Manfred Halpern, *The Politics of Social Change in the Middle East and North Africa* (Princeton, 1963), a pioneering work which provides rare insight into the pattern of social change; Albert Hourani, *Minorities in the Arab World* (London, 1947), though written during the last war is still extremely valuable; Daniel Lerner, *The Passing of Traditional Society: Modernizing the Middle East* (New York, 1958), provides the first rigorous sociological analysis of the modern Middle East; Bernard Lewis, *The Middle East and the West* (Bloomington, 1964), gives a concise, lucid analysis of the process of "westernization."

COLLECTIONS OF SPECIAL ESSAYS

Some of the best of the shorter essays written in the last fifteen years are included in the following three books: Sydney N. Fisher (ed.), *Social Forces in the Middle East* (Ithaca, 1955); Tibor Kerekes (ed.), *The Arab Middle East in Transition* (New York, 1958), and Richard Nolte (ed.), *The Modern Middle East* (New York, 1963).

SURVEYS OF NORTH AFRICA

Reliable works in English are few; for a general introduction, Nevil Barbour (ed.), *A Survey of North West Africa* [The Maghrib] (rev. ed.,

London, 1962); for a brief treatment of recent political developments, I. William Zartman, *Government and Politics in North Africa* (New York, 1963); and for the best survey to date, Charles F. Gallagher, *The United States and North Africa* (Cambridge, Mass., 1963). Three works in French are basic: Jacques Berque, *Le Maghreb entre les deux guerres* (Paris, 1962), a masterly analysis; Roger Le Tourneau, *Evolution politique de l'Afrique du nord musulmane, 1920-1961* (Paris, 1962), perhaps the best political survey to date; and Jean Lacouture, *Cinq hommes et la France* (Paris, 1961), an extremely readable work dealing with five major leaders of contemporary North Africa.

ISLAM AND ARAB NATIONALISM

On the development of Islamic law the most comprehensive is J. N. D. Anderson, *Islamic Law in the Modern World* (New York, 1959); Kenneth Cragg, *The Call of the Minaret* (New York, 1956), offers accurate and sympathetic insight. For two scholarly studies on the crisis of modern Islam, Gustav von Grunebaum, *Modern Islam: The Search for Cultural Identity* (Berkeley and Los Angeles, 1962), and Wilfred Cantwell Smith, *Islam in the Modern World* (Princeton, 1957). The ideas and political development of Arab nationalism are discussed in Hazem Z. Nuseibeh, *The Ideas of Arab Nationalism* (Ithaca, 1956) and in Walter Z. Laqueur, *Communism and Nationalism in the Middle East* (New York, 1956); translations from Arabic sources on Arab nationalism are found in Sylvia Haim, *Arab Nationalism* (Berkeley and Los Angeles, 1962).

SPECIAL STUDIES

Douglas Ashford, *Political Change in Morocco* (Princeton, 1961), provides a detailed study of the emergence of modern Morocco; Gabriel Ardent, *La Tunisie d'aujourd'hui et de demain* (Paris, 1961), is one of the best studies on Tunisia; Albert Hourani, *Syria and Lebanon* (London, 1946), is still the best treatment of the subject; Majid Khadduri, *Independent Iraq: A Study in Iraqi Politics, 1932-1958* (London, 1960), and *Modern Libya: A Study in Political Development* (Baltimore, 1963), are the standard authoritative works on the two countries; John Marlowe, *The Persian Gulf in the Twentieth Century* (New York, 1962), provides, in addition to a survey of political developments, a comprehensive treatment of the Middle East oil industry; F. Perroux (ed.), *L'Algerie de demain* (Paris, 1962), is one of the best works on Algeria; H. St. John B. Philby, *Saudi Arabia* (New York, 1955), is perhaps the last intimate glimpse, from the inside, of a traditionalist patriarchal society; Nadav Safran, *Egypt in Search of Political Community* (Cambridge, Mass., 1962), is a capable interpretive study; William Polk, *The United States and the Arab World* (Cambridge, Mass., 1965), is a sound analytical survey of both internal developments and U.S.-Arab relations.

DOCUMENTARY COLLECTIONS

J. C. Hurewitz, *Diplomacy of the Near and Middle East, A Documentary Record* (Princeton, 1956), 2 vols., concentrates on diplomatic developments and international relations; Muhammad Khalil, *The Arab States and the Arab League* (Beirut, 1962), 2 vols., includes important material translated for the first time from the Arabic; Helen Miller Davis, *Constitutions, Electoral Laws, Treaties of States in the Near and Middle East* (Durham, 1953), is still useful.

PERIODICALS

The Middle East Journal and *Oriente Moderno* are indispensable; the *Muslim World* and the *Middle East Forum* often include valuable material; for North Africa, the daily Parisian *Le Monde* and the weekly *Jeune Afrique* provide perhaps the best current coverage; the reports of the American Universities Field Staff include some of the best reporting on North Africa in English.